FATAL LUNCH

THE DEATH CAP MUSHROOM MURDERS

CHERYL WARREN

The names of certain individuals have been changed to protect their privacy in accordance with court suppression orders. Please see the Author's Note for details.

Cover design by Steven W. Booth / Genius Book Services

Cover photograph © Joel Carrett / AAP Photos

Edited by Leya Booth

ISBN: 978-1-7646299-0-4

A catalogue record for this book is available from the National Library of Australia.

First published in Australia.

AUTHOR'S NOTE ON PRIVACY AND ACCURACY

Extensive research has been undertaken to ensure the accuracy of the events described in this book. Every effort has been made to verify facts and timelines against multiple credible sources, including court proceedings, trial testimony and exhibits, legal documents, interviews, and contemporaneous media reports.

However, given the volume of coverage this case has attracted — and occasional inconsistencies between sources — minor discrepancies in dates or details may exist. Where sources were found to conflict, the author has prioritised court testimony and official legal records. Any errors or omissions are unintentional.

The names of Erin Patterson's children have been changed to comply with court suppression orders. The name of another child has been changed given he is a minor. Some individuals — including extended family members, Erin's online friends, and other peripheral figures — are referred to by first name only. This has been done deliberately to protect the privacy of ordinary people who have found themselves caught up in these terrible crimes through no fault of their own. All key figures central to the case are referred to by their full names.

Spelling and grammatical errors in text messages and other communications have been reproduced as they originally appeared.

CONTENTS

For my husband — first reader, honest critic, and the most patient man I know.

PROLOGUE

ON A CHILLY SUNDAY morning in late July 2023, four people woke up dying. They just didn't know it yet.

The previous afternoon, in a modern two-storey home on the outskirts of Leongatha — a small town in the green hills of rural Victoria — Erin Patterson had served lunch to her guests. Beef Wellington. Individual portions, golden-crusted and carefully plated. There were mashed potatoes. Green beans. A hostess who seemed happy to see them.

They were family. Don and Gail Patterson, married for decades, parents of Erin's estranged husband, and Gail's sister Heather and her husband Ian, the pastor of the local Baptist church. They had come because they were invited, and because that's what families do.

Hidden inside each pastry was *Amanita phalloides*. The death cap mushroom. Among the most lethal fungi on earth. A couple of mouthfuls of contaminated food are all that is needed. The toxin attacks the liver in silence, hidden behind symptoms easily mistaken for a stomach bug. By the time doctors recognise what they are dealing with, the damage is almost always fatal.

After her guests left, Erin went upstairs and played Lego. That evening, she took her son to Subway to buy dinner. It was an ordinary Saturday night.

By midnight, the vomiting had started. Within 24 hours, all four guests were in hospital. A week later, three were dead.

This is a meticulously researched account of what happened at that lunch and why. It goes deep into the history of how the diners came to be at the table, and examines the question at the heart of it all: How do you sit across a table from people who thought of you as family, and watch them eat something you know will kill them?

ACT I — THE LUNCH & THE PEOPLE

1 THE LUNCH

THE BUTTER-YELLOW WEATHERBOARD church sat at the top of a hill in a quiet residential area, its heritage red and green trim neat against the pale paint. Low shrubs and a closely mown lawn separated the building from the footpath.

It was Sunday, 16 July 2023. The morning service at Korumburra Baptist Church had just finished, and the congregation was spilling into the cool, slightly overcast winter morning. Pastor Ian Wilkinson had delivered that day's sermon. Inside, his nephew by marriage, Simon Patterson, was packing equipment at the sound mixing and laptop desk.

Simon's estranged wife, Erin, approached him while he was working. She told him she had a health issue she needed to discuss and wanted advice on how to break it to the children. She was inviting his parents, Don and Gail, along with Ian and his wife, Heather, to lunch to discuss this news. Would he be able to come?

Simon suggested morning tea instead. Erin was firm. She wanted it to be lunch. Simon agreed to attend.

She prompted him to put the commitment in his phone's calendar so he wouldn't forget. Simon later recalled, "I said, 'I don't really use it. I keep a paper diary at home and I'll write it down in the diary at home.'"

Outside, Erin caught up with her mother-in-law, Gail, and Gail's sister, Heather. She repeated the invitation. Heather, who had not yet seen Erin's new home, accepted at once. Gail felt a flicker of concern. Erin had been updating her about recent doctor's visits, including a needle biopsy and an MRI, and now she had, in her words, some important medical news to share.

Gail later marked the date in her diary: "Lunch at Erin's w Heather + Ian."

Saturday, 29 July — the day of the lunch — dawned cool and still. The region had been experiencing a dry spell, and the morning broke clear, a weak winter sun lifting the temperature to 18°C by late morning. For South Gippsland in July, it was almost warm.

Travelling together in Don's car were four of Erin's guests: Don and Gail Patterson, along with Heather and Ian Wilkinson. They arrived promptly at 12:30 p.m. To Erin's annoyance, Simon had declined the night before by text, saying he felt "too uncomfortable" — just as he had when she'd invited him to lunch the previous month.

Gail and Heather each brought something to share after lunch. Gail had baked an orange cake, a firm family favourite that she made often, and Heather brought a fruit platter. Erin's children — Ben, fourteen, and Kate, nine — were not at the house by the time their grandparents arrived. Erin had dropped them into town earlier so they could have McDonald's and enjoy a movie with a friend. Anyway, this lunch was for the adults.

Erin rarely hosted social gatherings. During her and Simon's marriage, family events were almost always held at his parents' place, or at his brother Matt's.

Erin met her guests at the front door, exchanged pleasantries, and then showed them inside. She hadn't dressed up. She wore a red windcheater, off-white pants, socks, and sandals — the same sort of outfit she wore almost every day, regardless of the weather or the occasion.

The ground floor was furnished simply. The dining area was framed by a large double sliding glass door that let in the midday light and looked out onto the side balcony. An old, overstuffed modular lounge suite sat on the balcony just outside the door, obscuring the view of the carport and garden beyond. A wooden table with matching light brown chairs for six sat in the centre of the dining room. The kitchen and breakfast bar were to the left. A dog bed lay by the door. To the right of the table, a shelf was cluttered with books and a scattering of knick-knacks. The room felt practical and lived-in.

When they reached the kitchen, Heather, a keen cook, asked to see the pantry. Erin opened the pantry door briefly but reluctantly, then ushered her guests outside for a tour of the garden. Heather assumed Erin's reticence stemmed from her pantry being untidy, but when this small, ordinary moment resurfaced later in Ian Wilkinson's testimony, the prosecution highlighted it as potentially more significant.

Back inside, the conversation settled around the

kitchen as Erin prepared the meal. She rebuffed offers of help as she finished the vegetables and plated the food, keeping her guests on the dining room side of the breakfast bar while she worked.

The main dish was beef Wellington.

Erin sourced the recipe from her copy of *RecipeTin Eats: Dinner*, Nagi Maehashi's best-selling cookbook. In the book, the recipe is accompanied by a photo of a single beef tenderloin log wrapped in pastry. But Erin made several changes. Since Don didn't eat pork, she skipped the prosciutto. She swapped the egg crepe for store-bought filo pastry as the crepe "looked a bit complicated." She said she couldn't find a suitable log of beef tenderloin, so used individual steaks purchased from her local supermarket. She prepared the beef Wellington as single-serve, pastry-style parcels — six in total. One for each of her four guests, one for herself, and one for Simon — despite his withdrawal the night before. The meal was accompanied by beans, mashed potatoes, and a gravy made from canned Gravox granules.

Erin placed the meals on the breakfast bar. Gail and Heather each picked up two plates and carried them to the table.

Ian took the seat at the head of the table, nearest the sliding glass door, with Don and Gail to his right and Heather to his immediate left. Erin sat beside Heather. Before eating, Ian led the group in saying grace. The meal itself was uneventful. The conversation flowed, and the food was well-received. Ian and Heather finished their portions. Gail ate half of hers. Don ate his, along with Gail's leftovers. Accounts differ on how much Erin ate. "A third," "half," and "most of" have each been offered by Ian and Erin at various times.

Gail's orange cake and Heather's fruit platter were brought out, though little of either was eaten. Everyone was quite full from the main course.

After the meal, the plates were set aside, and the conversation turned serious. Erin told the group that she had received the results of recent medical tests. Ovarian cancer. The words hung heavily in the air. Erin described the situation as serious. Potentially life-threatening. She was anxious and didn't want to worry the children. She asked the group for guidance on how to approach her diagnosis with the children. Don spoke for them, suggesting that honesty was best.

At 2:45 p.m., Simon dropped Ben and his friend Baldwyn back at the house. Daughter Kate stayed in the car and went home with Simon for the afternoon. Before the boys came inside, Ian led a brief prayer for Erin's health and recovery. Once the boys entered, the conversation deliberately shifted back to lighter topics. Ben engaged his grandfather, Don, in animated chatter about his planned flying lesson the next day.

By 3:00 p.m., it was time for the visitors to leave. Ian had a church meeting to attend, and still had to finish preparing the next morning's sermon.

After the guests departed, Ben helped his mother clean up by moving the dirty dishes to the sink, ready for the dishwasher. He then went upstairs to play video games with Baldwyn.

Thirty minutes after her guests left, Erin made a brief trip to the Koonwarra Transfer Station (rubbish tip) near

Leongatha and disposed of some cardboard and other rubbish.

When she returned home, Erin went upstairs to build Lego. In the early evening, she dropped Baldwyn off at home in Korumburra, then drove to Subway, where Ben bought them dinner. At 9 p.m. Simon dropped Kate back home. It was an uneventful and routine evening.

At Ian and Heather's home, the couple went to bed around 10:30 p.m. Before they fell asleep, Heather abruptly got up and rushed to the laundry. Ian could hear her vomiting. He was soon overcome by the same intense waves of nausea. They both vomited throughout the night.

In the early hours of the following morning, Heather called her sister to discover that Gail and Don were also unwell. Something was very wrong. It was time to seek medical help.

2 THE GUESTS

KORUMBURRA IS fourteen kilometres from Leongatha. Both the Patterson and Wilkinson families lived, worked, and raised their children there. Sisters Heather and Gail had always been close, and their families shared similar values. Family and church sat at the centre of everything they did. They were decent, grounded people, well-known and deeply respected in their community.

Don and Gail, both 70, were enjoying their retirement years. They were still reasonably active and heavily involved in their church and volunteer work. They had four adult children — Simon, Matthew, Nathan, and Anna — and delighted in their grandchildren.

Don, a retired science teacher, had a curious mind and a fondness for building rockets with the kids. Each morning, he would walk down to the shops to buy his morning paper, greeting neighbours and having a chat along the way. He was inquisitive and intelligent — something he had in common with Erin — and over the years they had enjoyed long conversations on a broad range of topics. His wife of 50 years, Gail, was a considerate and gentle woman. A stay-at-home mother while their children were younger, she had worked as a school office administrator once they were older. An accomplished cook, Gail enjoyed passing her kitchen skills on to her grandchildren.

Heather, 66, and Ian, 70, were also deeply woven into the local community. Together they had four children: David, Luke, Ruth, and Elizabeth. Ian had been pastor of the Korumburra Baptist Church since the late '90s. Like her sister, Heather had prioritised her children when they were younger. Once they were grown, she had worked as an integration aide at the Korumburra Secondary College. She loved reading, and as a child was fond of Enid Blyton books. She was also a keen music lover who had even attended a Rolling Stones concert in her younger days. Heather's children inherited her love of music. All four had played in the band at Korumburra Secondary College during their school years.

Both sisters — Gail and Heather — had extensive histories of volunteerism, including teaching English to migrant women and supporting disadvantaged children through a learning assistance program.

From 2013 to late 2018, Don and Gail had worked as volunteer editors of the *Burra Flyer*, a quarterly community newsletter that kept Korumburra ticking along with community news, sporting club updates, and advertising for local businesses. Simon often contributed as a volunteer photographer. Gail had a couple of health issues that made the workload increasingly onerous, so after the 2017-2018 summer edition, they stepped back from the *Flyer*.

Erin took over as co-editor with another local, John. Simon continued to contribute photo content. In her first issue, Erin was effusive in her praise of Don and Gail for the time they'd put into the *Flyer* and for helping her and John settle into their new roles. Eighteen months and six editions later, Erin resigned. Her private view of the job was far less polite than she conveyed to the extended family. She told online friends that she'd spent her time as editor "bringing together articles by illiterate motherfuckers and turning them into something legible."

3 ERIN TRUDI SCUTTER

BORN in Adelaide on 30 September 1974, Erin Trudi Scutter was the second of two daughters born to Eitan and Heather Scutter. When Erin was three years old, her family relocated to the Melbourne suburb of Hampton, then later to leafy Glen Waverley. Life in Melbourne was good. Erin grew up in a middle-class, high-achieving, intellectually driven household — the kind where books filled every corner and curiosity was simply assumed.

Eitan held directorships with several companies, including in his home state of South Australia, while Heather was a widely published and well-respected academic at Monash University. She specialised in children's literature. Their older daughter, Ceinwen, went on to become an accomplished geologist specialising in volcanology and, in her spare time, a talented cake decorator. As adults, Erin and her sister appear to have led largely separate lives. Ceinwen did not attend Erin's trial or sentencing, and has not spoken publicly about the case.

Erin's recollection of her childhood sits uneasily beside

the memories of others. She has described her upbringing as one lacking love — a cold, robotic mother who *"shame-weighed"* her daughters weekly, and a father too timid to stand up to his wife. Although neighbours and others who knew the family acknowledge Heather as the stronger personality of the two, they remember Eitan and Heather as kind, family-oriented people. The contrast between Erin's account and the impressions of others would become a recurring feature of her life: two versions of the same story, rarely aligning.

Despite her comfortable upbringing, Erin seemed to struggle. She has described a lifelong battle with depression and low self-esteem, which is perhaps reflected in her difficulty finding a clear career path.

After graduating from high school, she completed a business accounting degree but worked in the field for only a brief time. Over the years that followed, she moved between different jobs and study plans, starting more than she finished. As recently as 2023, she secured a place to study nursing at Federation University. Upon acceptance, she immediately deferred and never began the course.

Erin's early adulthood was shaped by a mix of independence and a persistent undercurrent of low self-confidence. She wasn't isolated — she had friends and people she spent time with — but she often sat slightly outside the centre of things. Depending on who you speak to, she has been described variously as funny or humourless, warm or cold, sociable or insular — bright and engaging one moment, abrupt or withdrawn the next. But one descriptor remains consistent across accounts: intelligent. That intelligence became obvious in 2001, when she passed the demanding entrance test for Airservices Australia and joined a small intake of trainee air traffic controllers at Melbourne Airport.

Colleagues remember her as technically strong — someone who handled the academic components of the training well — but socially out of step. She rarely joined group activities and often seemed detached from the camaraderie that formed among the trainees. Behind her back, some of the other trainees began calling her "Scutter the Nutter." Her time with Airservices ended in November 2002, less than two years after she started, following accusations of irregularities in her timesheets.

In 2004, Erin made the papers — and not in a good way. She was involved in a single-vehicle accident that was, at the time, reported in straightforward terms: an unregistered car, 95 kilometres an hour in a 60 zone, a blood-alcohol reading almost three times the legal limit, and leaving the scene. In court she received a $1,000 fine and a two-and-a-half-year licence suspension. Years later, as journalists revisited her past, some outlets would characterise the incident far more dramatically, calling it "a drunken rampage." Serious as it was, the crash remained Erin's only encounter with the law before the fatal lunch.

In the same year as her accident, Erin moved into work that aligned more closely with her interests. She joined the animal management team at City of Monash, working on behalf of the animal charity RSPCA. It was there that she met a young man named Simon. From that point on, Erin's story would take a very different shape.

4 ERIN AND SIMON

COMPLEX WOULD BE a good word to describe Simon and Erin's relationship.

At City of Monash, Erin became part of an eclectic work social group whose style seemed to suit her. She was sharp and capable, and while she wasn't the most outgoing member, she fit into the group reasonably well. Simon Patterson, a civil engineer, was part of the group.

Both in their late twenties when they met, Simon and Erin were opposites. He was tall, while she was short. He was a country boy, and she was a city girl. He was outgoing and warm, while she was more reserved and uncomfortable in crowds. But they got on well and enjoyed each other's company. Simon was drawn to Erin. He thought she was very intelligent and could be quite witty.

Simon and Erin's relationship progressed quickly, and they began dating the following year. During this period, Erin underwent an unexpected shift in her long-held atheist views after attending a sermon delivered by Simon's uncle, Pastor Ian Wilkinson. She later described the experience as a moment of sudden clarity that left her newly enthusiastic about Christianity, and the two soon began attending Bible study sessions together.

Simon and Erin became engaged in February 2007 and married on 2 June the same year at the Korumburra Anglican Church. They chose the Anglican Church so that Ian could attend as a guest rather than officiate, as he would have at the Baptist Church. Simon's cousin, David, walked Erin down the aisle. Her parents did not attend. Erin's explanation was that they were on holiday, travelling in Russia by train.

Around this same time, Erin began receiving regular distributions from her late grandmother's estate. According to Simon, she was drip-fed something in the order of $2,000,000 in periodic instalments that continued through to 2015.

The financial windfall gave the newly married couple an extraordinary sense of freedom, arriving at a time in their relationship when neither of them was especially money-driven. Beyond the obvious comfort it provided, they weren't motivated by wealth. This was reflected in how Erin lent hundreds of thousands of dollars to Simon's siblings to help them buy property. Although she would have been entitled to charge interest on these loans, she didn't. The loans were indexed only to inflation, and the repayment terms were equally generous: payments could be made when they could afford them, at a rate of their own choosing. In hindsight, those loans also created a quiet imbalance. Whether or not Erin intended it, lending such large sums placed her in a position of influence over her in-laws — a dynamic that would come to matter later.

Using their newfound financial freedom, Simon and Erin quit their jobs and travelled. They went on a trip to Africa. "We went camping through Namibia," Erin said. On their return home, they purchased camping gear and set off on a cross-country adventure. An avid photographer, Simon shared many photos online of perfect starry nights in the outback.

By the end of 2007 they had settled in Perth, where Simon secured work with a local council. Erin wanted to start a family. Simon would have preferred to keep travelling.

Their son Ben was born in Perth in early 2009. Erin described the birth as long and traumatic, ultimately requiring an emergency caesarean. It was the first documented instance of her signing herself out of hospital against medical advice. She distrusted doctors, disliked hospitals, and didn't want to stay. At the same time, motherhood felt overwhelming. In her own words, she wasn't prepared for the responsibility of a newborn. A couple of weeks after the baby was born, Don and Gail travelled to Perth to meet their grandson, and to support the new parents. They stayed almost two weeks. There was none of the tension that sometimes occurs when a well-meaning grandmother gives advice to a first-time mother. To the contrary, Erin was very grateful for Gail's presence. She praised how patient and supportive Gail had been during a time when Erin felt hopelessly out of her depth with her newborn son.

It wasn't long though before wanderlust returned for

the young couple. In April, with their new baby in tow, Erin and Simon packed the four-wheel drive, loaded their camping gear, and headed north. They slowly made their way toward Far North Queensland.

They reached Townsville in November. By then, Erin had had enough. Whether it was the shifting dynamic between her and Simon, the strain of caring for a newborn in a tent, postpartum depression, or a combination of all three, something had clearly changed for her. Whatever the cause, it was in Townsville that Erin left Simon and the baby and flew back to Perth alone.

It took Simon a week to drive himself and Ben back to Perth, by which time Erin had already secured a rental property for herself and their son. After less than three years of marriage, this was their first separation. Simon found the whole situation bewildering. Raised in a deeply religious family, he had always expected his marriage to be enduring and stable, something built to last. Erin offered no explanation for wanting to separate. Holding on to the possibility of reconciliation, he moved into an onsite caravan nearby.

His hopes were not entirely in vain. Erin agreed to marriage counselling and, by the end of January 2010, they reunited. Only to separate several more times over the years that followed. Their life together lurched through attempts at repair, never quite finding firm ground.

Erin attributed their relationship problems to an inability to communicate. Simon saw it differently. He believed her mental health was a significant contributing factor. "She struggled a lot with mental illness, postnatal depression... I believe that's real," he said.

In 2011 the family moved to Quinninup, south of Perth. Leaning into her strong interest in literature, Erin opened a small second-hand bookshop in nearby Pemberton. She had spent months collecting stock, travelling around Western Australia to book fairs, library sales, and estate clearances. Despite her passion, the shop was short-lived and closed within a year.

By late 2013, Erin was pregnant with their second child. After the complications and stress surrounding Ben's birth and early months, she and Simon agreed it was time to return to Victoria, closer to his family and their natural support network. Rather than simply fly home, they turned the move into one last outback adventure — five days crossing the remote 1,350-kilometre Anne Beadell Highway with their four-year-old son in tow. Simon documented the trip in an online blog, filling it with photographs of campsites beneath star-filled skies, little Ben playing cricket in the red dirt, a camel, and the ruins of a downed plane they had encountered along the way. "One of the greatest feelings in the world is camping under the stars in the Australian outback," he wrote.

Their second child, a daughter, Kate, was born in 2014, shortly after their return to Victoria. They bought a home in Korumburra, settling close to Simon's parents and siblings. During this time, Simon's sister, Anna, developed a strong bond with Erin. The two women were pregnant at the same time, and in a light-hearted family joke, their babies became known as "the twins," born just three days apart.

But the return to Victoria did little to ease the tension in Simon and Erin's marriage. Whatever the root cause, the unravelling wasn't sudden or seismic. Their relationship withered slowly and inevitably, ending once and for all in November 2015.

5 CHANGING RELATIONSHIP

IN THE YEARS after they separated, Erin and Simon's lives settled into a friendly coexistence. They shared parenting with relative ease, divided costs associated with the children without squabbling, and even took the occasional family holiday together.

Simon had helped his uncle set up a livestream of the weekly church service during COVID, and it had remained a fixture ever since. Simon managed the technical side, while Erin pitched in every couple of weeks to ensure it was running properly online.

For Simon, these small acts of cooperation kept alive a quiet hope that they might find their way back to each other. But whenever he gently raised the possibility, Erin made it clear that door was closed.

Through this period, as they always had, Simon's family continued to regard Erin as one of their own. She was invited to family events and remained in the family chat group on the messaging app, Signal. Don and Gail remained active in their grandchildren's lives. Don tutored Ben in maths.

Gail checked in on Erin from time to time, and Erin's replies reflected the same warmth, her tone affectionate and familiar.

In May 2022, Gail messaged via Signal, "Happy Mother's Day Erin. May God bless you. Love Don and Gail"

"Thanks Gail! Happy Mother's Day to the best mum-in-law anyone could ask for! xxoo," Erin replied.

Against this backdrop of family civility, Simon had begun experiencing a series of sudden, unexplained gastrointestinal illnesses.

The first was in November 2021. The night before a planned camping trip to Wilsons Promontory, he ate penne Bolognese that Erin had packed for him in a Tupperware container. "I couldn't tell you if it was a message or a phone call," Simon would later say, "but she encouraged me to have tea… and not wait too late." By morning he was vomiting. He was hospitalised overnight with severe, gastro-like symptoms. Erin was attentive, checking in and offering support.

Six months later, in May 2022, Simon and Erin took a camping trip to Howqua in Victoria's High Country. On the second night, 25 May, he ate a chicken korma she had cooked. By the following morning he was vomiting. He was treated at Mansfield Hospital and discharged, but days later his condition deteriorated sharply. Erin called an ambulance. Once he reached hospital, Simon was intubated and in intensive care for nearly three weeks. He underwent surgery and lost part of his bowel. Again, Erin was supportive. After a 24-day hospital stay followed by a further two weeks in rehabilitation, she invited him to recuperate at her home, even running errands and arranging vehicle repairs for him. But while he was staying with her, Simon fell ill again after a beef stew Erin had prepared. He was re-hospitalised for several days. Shortly after he returned to her home, Erin became irritated with Simon's lack of help around the house. She told him she wanted him to leave. He packed his things and went home.

On 6 September 2022, Simon and Erin did a redo of the previously aborted trip to Wilsons Promontory. Erin brought the food. For Simon, she had prepared a chicken curry wrap. Erin ate similar ingredients, "but they weren't in a wrap." Simon soon became ill. Again. This time, in addition to nausea and vomiting, he began to lose muscle function. He suffered a seizure in the ambulance, and was documented as being in a "reduced conscious state." This time when he was discharged, Erin drove him to his parents' home.

By now, Simon was starting to wonder. He changed his medical power of attorney from Erin to his father, Don, and his brother, Matt. Just to be cautious.

In November he told his father he suspected Erin was tampering with his food. Don listened carefully, then replied, "I suggest you don't tell too many people about that." They moved on to other things.

A little while later, Erin gave Simon a batch of cookies, telling him they had been baked by their daughter Kate.

She called him several times to ask whether he had eaten any of them. Simon found the repeated calls unsettling. He eventually took a tentative nibble of one, found the taste peculiar, so threw the rest away.

By February 2023, with the relationship between them continuing to cool, Simon's unease had grown enough for him to confide his concerns to his doctor. During a lengthy consultation on 21 February 2023, he told his general practitioner, Doctor Christopher Ford, what he had noticed.

In the absence of anything definite to support or refute what Simon had shared, Ford suggested he compile a spreadsheet of everything he ate and any symptoms he experienced — a practical step should he fall ill again. Simon wanted to avoid the 'if,' and quietly resolved never to eat Erin's cooking again. This precaution later explained his withdrawal from multiple lunch invitations that Erin extended to him over the ensuing months.

Simon held no such reservations for his parents. He had no reason to. On 24 June 2023, Don and Gail dined with Erin and the children at her Leongatha home. Simon had been invited too, but declined. He texted, "Hi Erin. Thank you for your kind lunch invite, together with mum and dad. I'm sorry, I'll decline, as I feel too uncomfortable about it."

He didn't offer what 'too uncomfortable' meant, and Erin didn't ask.

His parents went without him, and the lunch passed without incident. His suspicions, such as they were, remained focused on himself. And even then, doubt lingered. Perhaps it had all been a horrible coincidence. But he was cautious. He didn't want to get sick again. And conversations between him and Erin were increasingly prickly these days, particularly after the recent tax misunderstanding.

6 THE TAX MISUNDERSTANDING

IN LATE OCTOBER 2022, Simon dropped Kate back to Erin's Leongatha home after having her for a visit. Erin came outside. She looked unhappy. She wanted to speak to him.

Erin had discovered that Simon's accountant had listed him as 'separated' on his tax return. It was accurate — they had been living apart since November 2015. But for seven years, neither had formally notified government agencies of their separation. During that time, Erin had been claiming family tax benefits at the rate for intact households — around $15,000 per annum. She later explained the arrangement in a message to the family chat group, "We were basically lying to the government, telling them that we were a family with shared finances so they wouldn't make him pay child support."

Now that Simon's separation status was officially recorded, those payments would be adjusted downward. Significantly.

Simon offered to contact the tax office and say it was a

mistake. Erin dismissed the idea. That would be the perfect way to attract unwanted attention. The damage had been done. Whatever had prompted the change — an honest accounting error, or Simon quietly deciding after seven years that it was time to establish some formal distance — the result was the same. Erin's benefit payments would change, and their informal financial arrangement was over.

"She was upset about it," Simon later testified.

It was, on the face of it, an odd grievance for Erin to nurse. She was not a woman in financial difficulty. From the estate of her grandmother, and later her mother, she had received inheritances that ran into millions. After her arrest, the media widely described her as an heiress. Yet here she was, angry about the loss of government entitlements that, by her own account, she wasn't entitled to anyway.

She applied for child support through the government department, Services Australia. She complained to online friends, "His mum was horrified that I had claimed child support. Why isn't she horrified her son is such a deadbeat that I had no choice?"

The formal assessment came back. Simon was required to pay Erin $38 a month. Erin was deeply unhappy.

Around this same time, another incident added to the strain.

Don had organised a lunch at the local pub to celebrate Gail's 70th birthday. The day before the lunch, Simon texted Erin, "Dad mentioned he thought he'd asked you and you'd said yes... I mentioned it to the kids the other day and they hadn't heard about it."

Erin replied that the invitation felt like an afterthought, and she might pass. "What I reckon is that everybody forgot to invite me to this… I feel very hurt about that." He asked her to consider his mother's feelings.

Erin later acquiesced and attended with the children. But things between her and Simon didn't go smoothly. After the lunch, Erin messaged him to apologise for shouting at him earlier in the day.

The money issues between them dragged on. On 22 November Erin sent Simon a $360 anaesthetist's bill for a medical procedure Ben had recently undergone. He replied that Services Australia had instructed him not to pay anything for the children outside his assessed child support, "So I cannot pay that, I'm afraid."

Erin used the family chat group on Signal in an effort to have Don and Gail intercede with Simon on her behalf. In a series of long messages, she wrote, "Simon seems to be under the misapprehension that a child support assessment covers every expense for the children under the sun." Don replied, gently suggesting the two of them pray together.

Posting as 'ErinErinErin', she vented to her online friends. "I thought his parents would want him to do the right thing, but it seems their concern about not wanting to feel uncomfortable and not wanting to get involved in their son's personal matters are overriding that so fuck 'em." And then, "This family, I swear to fucking god." She went on to accuse Simon of gaslighting her, and his parents of using "weasel words."

Later, she added, "I suspect the best thing I can do is

just to forget about all of them and live my life. Simon is probably loving how upset I am about all this."

The messages were impulsive and ugly. At the time of writing she had no idea she would eventually have to account for them. Publicly, and at length.

School fees became another flashpoint. Under their previous arrangement, Simon had paid half of the not insignificant fees for the private school their children attended. Now he refused to contribute outside the assessed amount. Erin told her online friends that if Simon wanted to "walk away from his responsibilities," it was on him. "Maybe it's easier if he's not involved in even paying their school fees. It means I can choose their school all by myself and don't have to refer to him." She soon did exactly that. She pulled the kids out of the private school and enrolled them in a new school over an hour's drive from home. She listed herself as the sole parental contact. It was Simon's turn to be annoyed. Apart from the fact that Erin hadn't consulted him, at the very least he wanted to be acknowledged as father on his children's school enrolments.

Erin invited Don and Gail to her home to discuss her issues with Simon. It achieved little.

Simon texted Erin the following day, "Mum and dad told me you asked them over to yours yesterday. I understand there are two main issues. 1- How Ben is going 2- Finances for our kids."

He went on to say he had re-read the messages Erin had sent his parents in the family chat group. He noted the financial issues were "very emotive now." Simon suggested involving a mediator. The back-and-forth between Erin and his parents was getting nowhere, and the tone — from his perspective — had become increasingly hostile.

Erin's messages in the family Signal group were causing Gail stress, so she stopped reading them.

Ben began pulling back from his father. In his police interview, Ben said he and Kate had previously stayed with Erin during the school week and with Simon every weekend. However, more recently, Ben had stopped going to his father's house on weekends. He rarely saw Simon outside church or youth group now. The reason wasn't clear — whether it was teenage independence, the increasing tension between his parents, or something else — but the distance was noticeable.

By the time the New Year arrived, Simon and Erin's relationship had noticeably changed. The previously chatty text messages had dried up. The warmth between them had evaporated. Her relationship with her in-laws had changed too.

The goodwill was gone.

7 FOREVER HOME

USING money that she inherited from her mother's estate, Erin purchased a one-hectare semi-rural block of land in 2019. She was genuinely thrilled, telling her online friends, "I'm so excited I can't breathe."

Since returning from Western Australia, Erin had lived mostly in Korumburra. Simon's town. His parents' town. His church. His community. Even after their marriage ended, she was still living inside his orbit.

The home in Leongatha wasn't just a property. It was hers. Her own design. Her own front door. Fifteen minutes down the road from Simon and his family. Far enough for her own space. Close enough for the children — and for her — to remain part of the family.

Construction was completed in June 2022, and Erin and the children moved into her newly built home at 84 Gibson Street, Leongatha.

Situated 135 kilometres southeast of Melbourne, Leongatha is a small town of just under 6,000 people, set in the rolling foothills of the Strzelecki Ranges.

In winter the town reads as a study in muted tones: bare-leafed trees waiting for spring, low mist that settles in the hollows, and a cool grey-blue light that flattens distance and obscures detail. The South Gippsland Highway runs past wide green fields; in the fog, sheep and cattle become soft, breathing shapes, their warm breath steaming in the cold air.

The town runs on farming — beef cattle and dairy mostly. Wide streets connect a scattering of shops, services, and community facilities spread across a generous layout. Houses sit well back from the road. There is a sense of space here that you don't get in the city.

The township has a quiet beauty about it. A mix of rural charm and natural serenity that makes the place feel both peaceful and deeply connected. A low-crime, everyone-knows-everyone energy. Unremarkable. Friendly. Unhurried. Paradise, really.

Erin's home stood at the end of a dirt road — rendered brick and weatherboard, ringed by eucalyptus trees that dropped a steady carpet of leaves onto the roof and into the gutters. A wide dirt driveway led to a prominent double carport with a Colorbond roof. Gravel paths wound between newly planted garden beds, their soil still loose, and a fire pit surrounded by a scatter of low chairs sat in a far corner of the backyard.

Erin was proud of her finished home. It was perfect — peaceful and in a gorgeous location. She even had a couple of sheep as low-cost lawnmowers. As she put it, "I wanted it to be a house where the children would grow up, where once they moved away for uni or work, they could come back and stay whenever they liked, bring their children, and I'd grow old there. That's what I hoped for."

8 ONLINE LIFE

ERIN HAD BEEN FASCINATED by true crime for years. Her interest began with books, then deepened through podcasts she listened to almost constantly. One witness later described true crime podcasts as the backdrop to Erin's day, playing while she cleaned the house and ferried the children in the car. From there, moving into online forums where cases were discussed in real time was a natural progression. By 2018, she was already a member of several true crime chat forums, including the 'Keep Keli Lane Behind Bars' Facebook group, which had formed amid renewed public interest in the conviction of Sydney woman Keli Lane for the murder of her newborn daughter. The group — eventually more than 2,000 members strong — became a hub for intense debate as the case resurfaced through a major ABC podcast and documentary series.

Although Erin had been online for years, she had mostly been an observer. In her early days she was more likely to play *Farmville* — a simple, social farming game

— than chat. But during the COVID pandemic she became more active. In the isolation of lockdowns, special interest groups — including true crime communities — flourished as a way for people to stay connected. Erin moved from watching to weighing in, offering sharp, often uncompromising opinions on cases like Keli Lane, the Greg Lynn High Country murders, and the kidnapping of Western Australian girl Cleo Smith. Her comments about Cleo's mother were especially harsh, drawing criticism from a number of other chat group members.

Although she contributed across several forums, she was especially active in the Keli Lane group. Despite her sometimes sharp tongue, Erin developed a reputation as something of a 'super sleuth', known for her research instincts, technical fluency, and knack for uncovering obscure details. As her involvement grew, she formed closer bonds with a small subset of the group.

Those friendships eventually led Erin and a small group of women, including Daniela and Jenny, to split away from the main Keli Lane forum. They formed a Facebook Messenger group where the tone of their conversations shifted noticeably. Their chats became more personal, more candid, and more emotionally intimate — balancing true crime with daily life — recipes, hobbies, husbands, frustrations, small victories, and whatever the day ahead held. Erin even shared photos of a dehydrator she had purchased in early 2023, and joked about whether supermarkets would let her dehydrate fresh produce before she paid for it.

For Erin, who had few close relationships offline, the group became her social anchor. Outside of these women, and Simon's extended family, she had little in the way of real-world friends or connections. In person, she was guarded and private. At local sports with the kids, she didn't mix with the other parents. According to one of the other mothers, Erin just sat on her phone in the corner and didn't speak to anyone.

Online, it was a different story. Erin chatted endlessly, shared opinions freely, and was generous with her time and attention. The internet gave her something the real world apparently didn't — an audience that made her feel welcome.

Not everyone in the true crime groups remembered her fondly though. Some later said she could be quite divisive at times — creating drama and playing people off against each other. In a later interview, one group member shared a suspicion that Erin used multiple fake accounts to bully other members who she was in conflict with. Although suspected, nothing was ever proven.

Even within her small, intimate chat group, cracks began to show. Erin expressed jealousy toward her sister and resentment toward Simon, whom she sometimes sarcastically referred to as "The Messiah."

Her friends agreed she was a devoted mother — that was never in doubt. But over time they noticed that some of her stories were difficult to reconcile with earlier details she had shared. There were smaller inconsistencies at first — ones that carried no drama or tragedy, but still didn't quite make sense. She criticised 'hubby's' domestic skills at a time when she and Simon had been separated for years. She sought advice after her cat had eaten something in the garden. She didn't have a cat. She periodically deleted accounts only to reappear under a new name — from Erin Patterson, to 'ErinErin', to 'ErinErinErin'. She never used a photo of herself as her avatar, preferring a variety of dark images, such as a cartoon witch on a broomstick.

Then there were the bigger claims. She told her online friends she had worked with Romanian orphans. She described a near-miss encounter with serial killer Ivan Milat. She said a former fiancé had died in a motorcycle accident and, more shockingly, she had been banned from the funeral. Individually, some of her stories were odd. Taken together, they formed a troubling pattern.

On 3 August, less than a week after the fatal lunch, Erin turned on her digital world with the same methodical energy she had once used to inhabit it. She closed various internet-based accounts, deactivated her Facebook, and wiped her browsing history.

For a woman whose life had revolved so heavily around the internet, the silence was deafening.

ACT II — THE UNRAVELLING

9 AN ORDINARY SUNDAY

LATE SUNDAY MORNING, 30 July, the day after the lunch, Ben came downstairs to find Erin sitting at the kitchen table sipping coffee. She told him she was feeling "a bit sick," so they wouldn't be going to church. He asked whether they were still going to his flying lesson. The airfield at Tyabb was over an hour's drive away. It was a long trip if she was unwell. He told her he didn't mind if they stayed home.

Yes. Of course they were still going. She didn't want to disappoint him.

Just after 2:30 p.m., Erin, Ben, and Kate loaded into the car.

Forty minutes into the drive, she stopped at a BP service station near Caldermeade. CCTV footage showed Erin pulling up near the entrance, leaving the children in the car, and walking inside. She headed directly to the bathroom and came out exactly nine seconds later. From there, she moved to the sandwich case, casually perused the food, and made her selections. She then went to a different aisle, selected a packet of gummy sours, paid for her purchases, and returned to the car. According to Ben, who was sitting in the front seat, this was the only stop they made on the way to Tyabb.

Erin would later dispute this. She claimed she'd been so unwell that she was forced to make an urgent roadside stop prior to reaching the service station. She said she had diarrhoea, and used the bushes as a toilet. She had cleaned herself as best she could with tissues, placed them in a dog poop bag, and put that bag in her handbag — intending to dispose of it at the next opportunity. That opportunity, she said, was the BP service station bathroom.

When they were almost to the airfield Erin's phone rang. It was Ben's flight instructor, calling to cancel. Bad weather. Annoyed, Erin turned the car around and headed for home.

On the return journey, she stopped at Outback Jack's, a popular roadside donut van near Koo Wee Rup. Erin remained in the car while Ben made purchases for the family. Dim sims and a hot dog for himself and his sister, and a coffee for Erin. There were no toilet facilities at the van.

Erin was wearing white pants. She had been in the bathroom for nine seconds.

Before they arrived home, Simon called. "Mum and Dad and Heather and Ian are all crook and have been admitted to hospital," he said.

Ben confirmed that as soon as they arrived back home, Erin rushed straight inside. He assumed she was going to the toilet.

Later that afternoon, Erin and the children pulled out the Monopoly board and played a game together.

According to Erin, she served the children fillet steak with mashed potatoes and beans for dinner that evening. Leftovers from the lunch. By her own account, Erin was unwell, and she already knew her lunch guests were in hospital with symptoms resembling food poisoning.

EARLIER THAT SAME SUNDAY MORNING, after vomiting through the night, Don called an ambulance for himself and Gail. Ian and Heather were no longer answering their phones, and Don was worried.

As he waited for the ambulance, Don called Simon. He told him he and Gail were unwell, and that he had an ambulance on the way. He asked Simon to check on Ian and Heather.

Simon called. No answer. He drove to their home.

By the time the ambulance arrived, Don was so unwell that he had to be stretchered to the ambulance. Clutching her stomach, Gail walked out herself. They were taken to Korumburra Hospital. Paramedics asked Don what he had eaten the day before. "Beef stroganoff." He was confused. He couldn't remember.

When Simon arrived at Ian and Heather's home, the front door was unlocked. He found Ian grey and struggling, barely able to lift himself from a chair. Heather was sitting on the couch with a bucket beside her, looking, as Simon later put it, "pretty crook."

He helped them into his car and drove them to

Korumburra Hospital. Advised that the hospital was at capacity, he then took them to Leongatha Hospital. During the car ride, Heather returned to something that had been bothering her since the lunch — the plates. She quizzed Simon on whether Erin was short of crockery, wondering aloud why Erin had served herself on a different plate from the ones she had given her guests.

Simon, Ian, and Heather arrived at Leongatha Hospital just before 11 a.m. Ian and Heather's symptoms were assessed as being consistent with food poisoning. The lunch came into focus. First the meat. Then the mushrooms. Despite medication, their vomiting and diarrhoea persisted.

Simon stayed with them until their daughter, Ruth, arrived. He then drove to Korumburra Hospital to check on his parents.

Nurse Lisa Shannon was with Don and Gail on the ward. Don was deteriorating fast. Anti-diarrhoea medication was making no difference. His blood pressure was dropping. His pulse was climbing.

Simon later described his father as hunched, his face discoloured. Struggling to speak. "His voice was strained... in a way that... he wasn't right inside." Late that afternoon Don and Gail were transferred to Dandenong Hospital, a large metropolitan facility better equipped to deal with their declining conditions. They arrived at 6:39 p.m.

Simon had spent most of the day at Leongatha and Korumburra hospitals, then most of the night at Dandenong Hospital. In his testimony, he said he only got about two hours' sleep that Sunday night.

10 FIVE MINUTES

ON MONDAY MORNING, 31 July, Erin got up, had her morning coffee, then dropped the kids at the school bus stop.

At 7:10 a.m. Dr Beth Morgan, the overnight registrar at Dandenong Hospital who had been treating Don and Gail through the night, called Dr Chris Webster, the doctor on duty at Leongatha Hospital. Her patients were far too sick for simple food poisoning. Bloodwork through the night had revealed alarming signs of liver injury, and after numerous consultations with toxicology specialists, the working diagnosis had shifted. They now suspected *Amanita phalloides*. Death cap mushroom poisoning.

Erin called Simon at 7:30 a.m. and told him she felt sick. He said he had spent most of the night at the hospital with his parents and suggested they talk later. She became indignant, telling him she wanted him to drive her to hospital. He suggested that she call an ambulance instead. He later said her reply was sarcastic. "'I'll sort out my own problems' or something to that effect."

Thirty minutes after her call to Simon she packed a black backpack and drove herself to Leongatha Hospital. The distance from her home was 2.7 kilometres. She arrived at 8:05 a.m.

Ian and Heather were still there, in the Urgent Care Centre, part of the hospital's emergency department. In light of Morgan's call, Webster was simultaneously trying to stabilise them and organise their transfer to Dandenong Hospital.

Cindy Munro, a nurse, took basic details from Erin — "I've got gastro" — and commenced observations. Webster, advised that a new patient had presented with gastrointestinal symptoms, came over to speak to her. It was soon apparent to him she was the fifth person from the lunch. He shared Dandenong Hospital's concerns that she and her lunch guests had been exposed to potentially deadly death cap mushrooms. He asked where she had got the mushrooms for the meal. "Woolworths," she said. One word.

It was in that moment, Webster later said, that he knew.

Leongatha is a small hospital. Erin was sitting in a chair within sight of the Urgent Care bay where Ian and Heather lay in open-curtain cubicles. She didn't ask to see them. "I don't know if she even acknowledged their presence," Webster said.

Webster left Erin and returned to Ian and Heather.

Kylie Ashton, Director of Nursing, brought paperwork to admit Erin for monitoring. Erin replied that she wasn't prepared to be admitted. With that, she stood up and moved toward the exit, her backpack still on her back. She was leaving.

Ashton moved between Erin and the door, trying to reason with her. She told Erin it was serious. Her life was at risk if she left. Erin was adamant. She had her car keys in her right hand. With her free hand, she reached the wall and pressed the button to open the automatic door.

Dr Veronica Foote came to the door. She warned Erin that she could become ill very quickly, and that it was not safe for her to drive. CCTV footage of this exchange shows Erin waving her hands. Animated. Stepping toward the door. Dr Foote told Erin she would need to sign a discharge against medical advice form. She signed it without reading it, then walked out into the car park. It was 8:10 a.m. Erin had been at the hospital for five minutes.

They told Webster Erin had left. “Fuck,” he replied.

Webster couldn’t believe it. Did she not understand the gravity of the situation?

He called Erin’s mobile phone. No answer. Over the next hour he called twice more. Still no answer. He left messages. She didn’t call him back.

By 9:25 a.m. he was frantic. She had been gone for over an hour. He needed police help. He called triple zero.

“This is Doctor Chris Webster calling from Leongatha Hospital,” he told the operator. “I have a concern regarding a patient who presented here earlier, but has left the building and is... umm... potentially exposed to a fatal toxin from mushroom poisoning. I have tried several times to call her on her mobile phone.”

He shared her home address. He spelled out her name. P-A-T-T-E-R-S-O-N. First name E-R-I-N.

Five people had eaten a meal on Saturday, he explained. Two were in intensive care. Two had just been transferred. Erin had presented that morning with symptoms of poisoning. While he was managing the critically ill patients, she had discharged herself against medical advice. "She left at... ten past… ahh… she was only here for five minutes," he said. The operator confirmed police had been notified and took Webster's number so he could be informed of the outcome.

Erin later said she had to go home to get prepared as she wasn't expecting a hospital admission.

11 THE RETURN

ERIN RETURNED to the hospital at 9:48 a.m. — just over an hour and a half since she had left. Paperwork was completed and she was settled into a bed in the Urgent Care Centre.

Her clinical notes indicated she was mildly dehydrated, and that her blood pressure and pulse were slightly elevated. Her symptoms were consistent with stress or anxiety, or mild gastric illness.

Doctor Webster came to speak to Erin. She told him she had eaten the same meal as her guests, and that she had given the children the leftovers for dinner the following night. Webster advised that they would transfer her to Melbourne. A metropolitan hospital would be better equipped to treat her if her condition deteriorated. The children would also need to be admitted for assessment. They may have been exposed to the same toxins.

Erin began to cry. This was unnecessary. She had scraped the pastry and mushrooms off. The children didn't need to be scared.

Webster replied, "They can be scared and alive, or dead." In court, Erin said she thought it was "a pretty bizarre thing for him to say."

She texted Simon. "They're arguing with me now saying I might have to go to Dandenong.... This doctor is not listening to me and is being a bit mean about it." She told him that she would get the children from school. He replied, "I'm glad you're feeling well enough to make the drive." Erin retreated. Simon could get the kids.

She did not ask after his parents, or his aunt and uncle.

Dr Conor McDermott, a toxicology registrar at Austin Hospital, phoned Erin while she was in Leongatha Hospital. He was calling on behalf of the Victorian Poisons Information Centre. He wanted to better understand what had happened. Erin conveyed the same information about the meal. She confirmed the source of the mushrooms was Woolworths, but added a new detail — that she had supplemented the Woolworths mushrooms with some she had purchased from a Chinese grocer in Oakleigh. McDermott googled a list of Asian food stores in Oakleigh, offering to read them out. She replied she wouldn't be able to recall even if he named the shop, then said it might have been in Glen Waverley anyway.

That afternoon, McDermott contacted the Victorian Health Department to share the details of a suspected poisoning event.

Police called Webster back. They were at Erin's home following up the welfare check prompted by his earlier triple zero call. He told the police that Erin was now at the hospital. He handed her the phone. She told police there were food scraps from the beef Wellington in a Woolworths shopping bag in the bin in her yard — the leftovers from the children's meal. She gave the police the gate code and permission to retrieve them.

Erin was transferred to Monash Medical Centre by ambulance shortly after 1 p.m. The journey took just over ninety minutes. During the trip, she complained of nausea and a sudden headache and was given fentanyl for the pain. She did not experience diarrhoea or ask to use the toilet during the drive.

At Monash, Erin was given IV fluids and N-acetylcysteine, a drug to protect her liver ahead of results from liver function tests. When the results came back, there was no sign of toxicity in her liver. As a precaution, further tests were ordered, including bloodwork.

She texted Simon, "I feel nauseous and sore tummy but they gave me ondansetron and saline and fentanyl."

Erin's medical observations in Monash were consistent with Leongatha's. Apart from chapped lips, Erin seemed largely well. On Monday evening Erin texted her sister-in-law — Matt's wife — to say she was in hospital and was feeling "nauseous, dizzy and tired."

By this time, Don and Gail had been transferred to the Austin Hospital. They were in a fight for their lives.

While Erin was in Monash, Professor Rhonda Stuart, Director of Public Health and Infection Prevention at Monash Health, came to speak with her. Erin reiterated what she had previously shared with McDermott regarding the meal, leftovers, and source of mushrooms. Stuart asked whether Erin had been foraging. She said no, and asked why she was being quizzed. Stuart explained that she was trying to establish whether there was a broader public health risk.

Ian and Heather had been transferred from Leongatha to Dandenong Hospital on Monday. But by Tuesday morning, their conditions had deteriorated significantly. Heather was transferred to Austin Hospital at around 1:30 p.m. She had multiple organ failure and was considered too unwell for a liver transplant. Ian arrived later that same afternoon, intubated and on mechanical ventilation. Acute liver failure had set in.

Erin was given the all clear and discharged from Monash on Tuesday afternoon. By then, all four of her lunch guests were critically ill in the intensive care unit of Austin Hospital.

12 THE GOOSE CHASE

THE HEALTH DEPARTMENT MOVED QUICKLY. Apart from the unusual nature of the toxin, its involvement was otherwise routine. When two or more people become ill after eating the same food, it is considered a community outbreak, and the department's role is to assess and reduce any potential risk to the wider public. In such cases, they have the power to issue food recalls and public alerts advising people to return questionable food for a refund.

Sally Ann Atkinson, manager of the Department of Health enterics team, was allocated to manage the investigation. Enterics, as she would describe it, covers "anything to do with vomiting, diarrhoea, gastro-type illnesses, things like salmonella, campylobacter, typhoid, Hep A, anything that causes a gastro illness."

Death caps were unprecedented territory for Atkinson. She had never handled an amatoxin poisoning before. She notified her manager and also contacted the food safety team — if there were poisonous mushrooms out in the community somewhere, they needed to find them. And fast.

Given two children were among the patients, a referral was also made to the Victorian Child Protection Service. On Tuesday morning, Child Safety Officer Katrina Cripps visited Monash Hospital with a colleague to speak with Erin, Simon, and their children.

When Cripps spoke to Erin alone, Erin offered her a graphic account of how ill she had been early Saturday evening — sick enough, she said, that she had barely managed the drive to drop Ben's friend home. Erin also confided in Cripps about the child support issues between her and Simon, and described Simon as controlling and emotionally abusive. She said he was someone who made her doubt herself as a parent and had worked to isolate her from his family.

When asked the purpose of the lunch, Erin explained she had simply invited the family because she missed them and wanted to reconnect. She also said something about a minor medical issue. There was no mention of cancer. The devastating diagnosis that had assembled four people at her table — the entire reason they had come — had been quietly abandoned.

Atkinson telephoned Erin later on Tuesday and asked about her symptoms. Erin replied that, although she was feeling much better now, she had become quite unwell around midnight on Saturday with "explosive diarrhoea." This timeline contradicted the "early evening" description she had given to Cripps during their meeting that morning.

Erin went on to explain that her condition had eased

on Sunday, enough for her to manage a small bowl of cereal at dinner time, but then had worsened again. After getting the kids off to school on Monday morning she decided she needed to go to hospital for treatment. She made no mention of her swift departure from the emergency department.

Atkinson took her to the source of the mushrooms. Erin said most of the ingredients for the meal were from Woolworths Leongatha, but that she had added some dried mushrooms she'd purchased back in April. When pressed about where she had bought them, Erin said it was an Asian grocery store. She couldn't recall where because, being school holidays, it was a time when she had "driven around a lot." It might have been somewhere in Clayton, or Oakleigh, or Mount Waverley.

Erin said the mushrooms were in a small clear plastic bag when she purchased them, that she had subsequently transferred them into a Tupperware container, and that she had discarded the original packaging. She said she had bought them for a pasta meal, but found them a bit pungent, so she set most aside for another time.

Her recent beef Wellington recipe called for one kilogram of mushrooms so, to make the meal a little more fancy, she had rehydrated the dried mushrooms from the Tupperware container and added them to fresh ones purchased from Woolworths. She said she had fed the lunch leftovers to the children the following night, though she had scraped the mushrooms off.

Atkinson debriefed her supervisor and the health department's media team. A wide-reaching mushroom recall was considered premature. What they needed was more information about the meal, including exactly where Erin had bought the dried mushrooms.

Once the meeting ended, she called Erin. No answer.

Atkinson sent Erin a text asking about the drinks served at lunch, the type of shallots used, and for more details about the plastic bag. She asked whether Erin could recall any street names or landmarks near the Asian grocery store she had visited. This detail would be crucial if they were to have any chance of finding the source.

Erin eventually replied, "Hi Sally. Sure i will try to get that information all to you as soon as possible… I'm just dealing with trying to manage and look after the kids in hospital here and a bit snowed under trying to manage that."

Erin didn't get back to her.

The next morning, Wednesday 2 August, Atkinson called again. No answer. She sent a detailed text:

1. *Can you please confirm that it was definitely only the one other time you cooked with the dried mushrooms when you first opened them? None else reported symptoms or issues when consumed then?*
2. *Please advise what drinks were served at lunch.*
3. *Please confirm what kind of shallots were used in the beef Wellington. Were they spring onions or the small individual shallot type onions please.*
4. *Did you possible use your card to purchase the mushrooms and can you please check your bank*

statements for the shop — that would be amazingly helpful.

No reply.

Four people were in hospital. They were critically ill. Erin's phone was working. She simply wasn't responding.

Atkinson knew that Cripps of the Child Protection Service had an appointment with Erin at 1 p.m. that afternoon. She asked Cripps to call her once she was with Erin.

That afternoon Cripps called from Erin's home. She handed Erin the phone. Now Erin had no choice but to speak to the health department.

The first contradiction came early in their conversation. Erin told Atkinson she was wrong about the pasta dish. She said that, because they smelled funny, she did not use any of the dried mushrooms in the pasta. The first time she had used them was in the beef Wellington. Atkinson was certain that during their very first conversation Erin had told her she had used some in the pasta dish, and had retained some.

Erin confirmed she had used small onion-type shallots, not spring onions, and that there was some leftover food at the house the health department was welcome to collect. On the question of the Asian grocery store, she could offer nothing more specific than a small suburban store in either Oakleigh or Clayton. Or perhaps Mount Waverley. She couldn't remember which. She couldn't remember any identifying features. She said the dried mushrooms had definitely been repackaged by the store, as there was handwriting on a white label on the bag.

In a desperate attempt to narrow down the location,

Atkinson asked whether Erin had perhaps visited a fast food drive-through or a coffee shop nearby. No. She asked whether Erin had ever foraged for mushrooms herself. Again, no. Erin confirmed she had cooked the beef Wellington in individual serving sizes rather than a log.

Atkinson contacted Monash City Council. An environmental health officer spent all day Wednesday and Thursday physically searching Asian grocery stores across the suburbs Erin had named. He went shop to shop, photographing dried mushroom products on shelves and sharing the images with Atkinson. Nothing matched Erin's description. No store carried anything resembling what she had described.

In an effort to prompt Erin's memory, Atkinson texted her the photos. Erin replied, "They weren't whole like those shitake mushies in the photos, they were sliced. And yes the packaging was about half the size of that."

On Thursday, Atkinson called Erin again. She asked about the mushroom duxelles — the paste used to coat the steaks. Erin described the dried mushrooms as sliced, and of a similar colour to the button mushrooms she had bought at Woolworths. Still hoping to narrow down the location of the Asian grocery store, Atkinson asked Erin to reconfirm the suburb. Erin said it was definitely somewhere in Oakleigh, Clayton, or Glen Waverley.

Glen Waverley.

This was new to Atkinson. In their previous conversations Erin had said Mount Waverley. There were more stores to check.

Despite intensive efforts, every lead came up blank. No other reports of illness had been received. No Asian grocery store matching Erin's description had been found. The investigation established it was "highly unlikely that the commercial food supply chain was contaminated with death cap mushrooms". Woolworths was in the clear.

By Friday 11 August, the Department of Health formally concluded its investigation. This was an isolated incident. The risk to public health was deemed very low.

13 BATTLE LOST

IT WAS Monday 31 July 2023 — just two days since the lunch. Don and Gail had been transferred from Korumburra to Dandenong Hospital the previous evening. Overnight, their conditions had deteriorated significantly. The death cap mushrooms were wreaking havoc on their livers. They needed to be transferred again – this time to the Austin Hospital — home to the Victorian Liver Transplant Unit. A transplant was their only hope of survival.

Don arrived at the Austin first. He was vomiting blood and his skin had taken on a yellowish cast. Acute liver failure had set in. Gail arrived later that evening. She was critically ill, in multiple organ failure, and was intubated — a breathing tube inserted through her mouth and into her windpipe, connected to a mechanical ventilator that breathed for her. The machine's steady hiss was the only sound in the room.

Ian and Heather were also transferred to the Austin the following day, Tuesday. By then Ian's condition was so grave that he had already been intubated before arrival.

Heather was conscious on arrival but deteriorating rapidly. By Wednesday morning her liver had essentially stopped functioning. An abdominal X-ray revealed gut ischaemia — the blood supply to her bowel had ceased. Despite doctors doing all they could to stabilise them, both Gail and Heather were deemed too unwell for a liver transplant.

Members of the extended Patterson and Wilkinson families had been at hospitals almost continuously since Sunday morning. By Wednesday they were deeply anxious, sleep-deprived, and mentally drained.

There is a small multi-faith chapel and prayer room on level two of the Austin Hospital. Open 24 hours a day, it is described as a space for private worship, prayer, reflection, and meditation. It was there, on Wednesday evening, that Simon gathered his siblings and several other close relatives. They sat together on black chairs arranged in a circle. For the first time, Simon shared his suspicions about Erin. They all knew he had been dangerously ill several times in 2021 and 2022, but now he told the full story — the camping trips, the food Erin had prepared, her strange insistence that he eat, and how he had eventually stopped eating anything she made — just in case. He explained these suspicions were the reason he had pulled out of the lunch. He apologised repeatedly. He felt the weight of guilt.

On Thursday morning he emailed his medical records to the family as proof. Shortly after, one of the Wilkinson family members contacted police and shared what Simon had told them.

Erin was also busy on Thursday. She moved a SIM

card from her Samsung tablet into a spare mobile phone. She disconnected from the Patterson and Wilkinson families by deleting herself from all family and private chats on the Signal chat application. She briefly re-joined the Keli Lane Facebook group under an assumed name, 'UnDeux-Trois Croissant'. But a short time later, she deactivated her Facebook account and scrubbed her online history. She was never seen on Facebook again.

On Friday 4 August, Don received a liver transplant. That same day, Gail and Heather died. In the same hospital, from the same poison. They had raised their children in the same town. They went to the same church. They died only hours apart.

That same afternoon, police retrieved a dehydrator from the Koonwarra rubbish tip.

Don's condition continued to deteriorate. Despite the liver transplant, his body could not fight any longer. He died late Saturday night.

What had begun as a food poisoning inquiry was now a murder investigation. Ian was still alive, still in intensive care. His survival was uncertain.

The Patterson and Wilkinson families released a joint statement. They paid tribute to Don, Gail, and Heather as parents, grandparents, siblings, and pillars of their community. The past week, they said, had been one of shock and grief.

14 SEARCH WARRANT

AT 11:40 a.m. on Saturday 5 August 2023 police arrived at Erin's home. It had been one week since the lunch. Detective Sergeant Luke Farrell introduced himself at the door. He told Erin they were investigating the deaths of two people. Erin asked, "Who died?" He told her that Gail and Heather had died the previous day. She expressed surprise. She didn't cry.

While Farrell coordinated the search, Detective Leading Senior Constable Stephen Eppingstall stayed with Erin.

The police team executed the search warrant with practised efficiency. Officers moved through the house in a steady rhythm. For close to four hours they opened cupboards, looked in drawers, lifted and photographed items. They seemed particularly interested in the kitchen, in anything that might be secreted in bedrooms, and in electronic devices. Among the things they seized were a recipe book, digital kitchen scales, and a gravy jug.

In Ben's room, they found an old Cooler Master

computer in the back of the wardrobe. In another bedroom, they found an old black Samsung phone that belonged to Erin, stashed in the wardrobe. It wasn't her day-to-day phone, but an older handset.

Every item was carefully catalogued and sealed into clear plastic evidence bags. The house was full of books. Hundreds of them. Lining shelves, stacked on surfaces, inside cupboards. Police would eventually catalogue over four hundred, though Erin later told the court she believed the number was considerably higher, as she still had unopened moving boxes full of books out in the garage.

Among the books police catalogued, there were a significant number of true crime titles. The jury would never hear about those titles though — the defence successfully challenged their inclusion during pre-trial argument. What they did hear about was the large number of books dedicated to various diets —a small detail, but one that spoke to a woman who, on her own account, had struggled with her weight and self-image for years.

The search went on.

Sometime in the early afternoon Erin asked Eppingstall if she could be alone to call her lawyer. He waited outside while Erin stepped into the lounge room and closed the door behind her. Twenty minutes later she emerged. She said nothing, but gave Eppingstall a polite smile.

The prosecution later presented evidence in court showing that a mobile phone owned by Erin was factory reset at 1:20 p.m. — during the police raid.

The search was completed just after 3:30 p.m.

Sitting across from Erin at her dining table, Farrell advised her there was one last item they needed to take. The warrant authorised them to take possession of her phone. She handed over a mobile phone in an orange flip case. Farrell cited a law that also required her to give him the PIN code for the phone. She offered two. Fiddling with the phone, he said, "Oh. It doesn't have a PIN." Erin replied, "Well, that makes your job easier."

She didn't tell Farrell it wasn't her usual phone.

He then advised Erin that they wished to interview her at Wonthaggi Police Station. She agreed. She didn't have to speak to police, but it would have looked a bit odd if she refused. After all, at this stage she was a witness, not a suspect — and witnesses are generally very cooperative.

She got into an unmarked police car and was driven the thirty minutes to Wonthaggi. Conversation was limited, if polite. At the station, the vehicle paused while electronic gates opened into a secure car park. She was escorted past marked and unmarked vehicles and in through the rear of the building.

15 FIRST INTERVIEW

THE INTERVIEW BEGAN at 4:47 p.m. In the interview room, the red light on the video recorder blinked steadily. Detective Eppingstall confirmed that Erin had been given an opportunity to speak to a lawyer before the interview, and was happy to proceed. He noted she could end the interview at any time. She agreed to continue.

He confirmed her personal details and asked for her phone number. She gave a number ending in **835**. That was her first lie. Her primary phone number — the one she'd used for hundreds of calls and over a thousand texts in the preceding months — ended in **783**.

"Following eating at your house... Donald, Ian, Gail and Heather all became so ill that they ultimately ended up in the intensive care unit at both the Dandenong Hospital and moved to the Austin Hospital. Umm, following that, they had umm... a deterioration in their condition and they became so ill that their livers have failed."

Erin nodded. "OK."

Stone-faced. Rapid blinking.

"Donald underwent a transplant last night," he continued, "and his condition is still extremely critical, and Heather and Gail have passed away."

A small shake of her head. No tears. No visible shock. Just a single slow blink.

"We're trying to understand what made them so ill," he said. "Conversely, we're trying to understand why you're not that ill."

Her eyes stayed fixed on the table, as though the wood grain was more compelling than the seriousness of what he had just told her.

"Hmmm. Yep," she replied. "But I'm sure you understand too, that I've never been in a situation like this before, and I've been very, very helpful with the health department through the week because I do want to know what happened. So I've given them as much information as they've asked for and offered up all the food, and all the information about where the food has come from."

She had avoided calls, ignored messages, and when she finally spoke to the health department, she had lied.

But Eppingstall didn't challenge her. She was there voluntarily. If he pushed too hard, she could end the interview and leave. So he let the lie sit between them and simply moved on.

Erin confirmed that, during the police search of her home, she directed police to the fruit platter and gravy, and the recipe book she used for the meal.

Eppingstall noted the lack of Asian ingredients in her pantry. She replied dryly that they should have looked in her fridge.

He shifted to mushrooms. The ingredient doctors had indicated as the most likely cause of the deaths. Had she ever foraged for them?

"Never!… Never!"

Her denial was emphatic.

Did she preserve foods? Own a dehydrator?

"No."

"Have you ever dehydrated food?"

"No."

He changed direction.

"I'd like to understand why you had Simon's parents and aunty and uncle over."

"Because they were the only" — she lifted her fingers in air-quotes — "'family' that I've got. They've always been really good to me, and I want to maintain those relationships, despite what's happened with Simon." She continued, "I think Simon hated that I still had a relationship with them... I loved them. Nothing that's ever happened between us. Nothing that he's ever done to me will change the fact that they're good, decent people who have never done anything wrong by me ever."

The bitterness she felt toward Simon was more visible here than she would later accept in court.

Still, Eppingstall didn't challenge her. He kept the steady cadence of his questioning.

He moved to the morning of 31 July, when Erin had presented at Leongatha Hospital. She had left after only five minutes. Why?

Her eyebrows lifted; her tone sharpened. "When you've got animals at home, and children who have multiple after-school activities, you can't just be told to drop everything and you're off to Melbourne overnight. So I had to go home and feed the animals, and pack my daughter's ballet bag. And I did that, and I went back."

She didn't mention the 90-minute gap. She didn't mention whether she'd had any fears for her own health.

She described her interaction with a Doctor Webster at the hospital. About him telling her he had two critically ill patients, and his concern about the possibility that they had ingested death cap mushrooms.

"I said, 'What?'" Erin recalled. Probed for more details, she couldn't remember whether this conversation happened when she first self-presented or when she returned to the hospital later that morning.

Eppingstall moved on without reacting.

She confirmed she'd been placed on a drip, possibly given liver-protective medication, then transferred to a larger hospital in Melbourne. He asked how long she had been hospitalised.

Overnight.

He told her that the police had warrants for the medical records of all people present at the lunch. Hers as well as her guests. She nodded.

Then came the list of seized items.

"Instruction manual for a Sunbeam Foodlab electronic dehydrator," he read. A pause. "What's that in relation to? Do you know anything about a dehydrator in your house?"

She denied owning one. She said she just collected manuals over the years. She couldn't recall ever owning a dehydrator. Perhaps years ago. She pivoted the conversation to her Thermomix and her enjoyment of cooking from scratch.

He let the deflection pass.

He continued down the list: the *RecipeTin Eats* cookbook, a set of digital kitchen scales, the fruit platter, the white gravy jug. Three computers from the study. An iPad from the lounge in a black and red case. Erin corrected him. It was a Samsung tablet.

Then, almost casually, "From Ben's room we grabbed a computer."

The shift was immediate. Erin's eyes widened — just for a moment — before she caught herself. She looked up toward the ceiling, closed her eyes, blinked rapidly, then gave a small, nervous laugh.

"Oh. Oh. That would be an old one that I had in the top of his cupboard. Yeah. Yeah. A very old one...."

It was the only moment in the interview where her composure slipped.

"So, if I had to prioritise, that would be bottom of the list?" he asked.

She closed her eyes momentarily, pursed her lips, and shook her head dismissively.

The contents of that old Cooler Master machine — the one stashed in Ben's wardrobe — would later become critical evidence at trial.

Further down the list, he noted two tablets from her bedroom and several mobile phones, including the phone she had handed over at the dining table. She didn't tell him it wasn't her primary phone. Instead, "Before you said a black mobile phone. That would be a Nokia. It's a really old thing." She said it was just a spare for in case she had to send her phone for repair.

Erin confirmed she had directed police to the leftovers in the bin on the morning she went to hospital. He thanked her for her assistance.

He asked if she had any questions. She didn't. The interview ended at 5:35 p.m. Police drove Erin home.

At 5:16 a.m. the following morning, Erin remotely factory reset the mobile phone she had given to police during the raid at her home the prior afternoon. At the time of the reset, it was sitting in an evidence bag in a police locker.

16 A SUSPECT IS DECLARED

TO DATE, the media had only limited details — a country lunch, three guests deceased, and a fourth very ill. The people who had died were said to be pillars of their community. It all sounded like a tragic accident.

But over the weekend, rumours had started to circulate through media circles that there was more to the story. Police sources had leaked the fact that, on Saturday, police had raided the home of the lunch host. The Homicide Squad was involved. Media interest increased immediately.

The police service needed to get on the front foot.

It was the morning of Monday 7 August. Standing at a lectern in front of a blue Victoria Police media backdrop, Detective Inspector Dean Thomas, head of the Homicide Squad, appeared before the assembled media. Grim-faced and serious, dressed in a dark suit jacket, checked shirt and tie, he read from prepared notes.

Homicide Squad detectives, he said, were investigating how four guests had become ill after attending a lunch at a Leongatha home on 29 July. Three of those guests had now died. He said the victims' symptoms were consistent with death cap mushroom ingestion. He was careful to note that Homicide Squad involvement did not necessarily mean foul play — but did confirm that police had interviewed the 48-year-old lunch host two days earlier.

At the conclusion of his statement, he took questions.

"Yes. She is," he replied, when asked whether the woman who hosted the lunch was a suspect. "And she was, and she is because she cooked those meals for those people who were present." He stumbled, but still chose his words carefully. "That woman has not presented with any symptoms, but we do have to keep an open mind in relation to this. It could be very innocent. But again, we just don't know at this point."

When asked whether charges were expected, he replied, "Not at this stage." There was still a great deal of work to do. They needed to understand what had caused the symptoms, what had caused the deaths. A fourth person remained in a critical condition in hospital. Toxicology testing could take some time. He couldn't give dates.

"But it's really interesting, you know," he volunteered. "Four people turn up, and three of them have passed away. And another one is critical. And we just need to work through this."

He confirmed that the woman interviewed by police over the weekend was the daughter-in-law of one of the couples. That she and her husband were separated, though he had been advised that the separation was amicable. They had two children together.

The deaths had already featured in the morning's

online news. The victims had been identified. Photos of Don and Gail, Ian and Heather accompanied the stories. Mushroom experts were suddenly in demand for sound bites. Images of death caps filled the papers. It was widely, but inaccurately, reported that the children had attended the lunch.

The media started chasing down leads. The Department of Health, mentioned by Thomas during the press conference, was contacted. They released a statement to confirm they were investigating, that enquiries were ongoing, and offering condolences to the affected families.

Given the identities of the lunch guests were now known, along with confirmation of the "48-year-old female" lunch host's connection to her guests, it didn't take the media long to identify Erin. As veteran Australian journalist John Ferguson later noted, "In terms of her, it was now pretty much game on."

And it was.

She returned from running errands later that day to find media waiting outside her gate. As Erin pulled into the driveway, they entered the property. Channel Nine reporter Sam Cucchiara was accompanied by a cameraman, a boom operator, and a female reporter.

Erin got out of the car. She was dressed for errands, not cameras — a grey knitted cowl-neck jumper, white track pants, white socks, and sandals. Her hair was messy. She slung her crossbody bag over her shoulder. The questions started before she had taken a step.

"Can you tell us about the meal you cooked?"

Cucchiara stepped forward. He was neatly dressed in a dark suit and tie, hands clasped behind his back.

Erin ignored his question. She wiped her eyes and removed her glasses. Speaking in a quivering voice, she said, "I'm so devastated by what's happened. The loss of Don… and Don's still in hospital. The loss of Ian and Heather and Gail, who were some of the best people that I've ever met."

She blinked rapidly. Just as she had two days earlier in the police interview. She did not look at Cucchiara. She looked off to the right.

"Gail was like…." A pause. Two long blinks. She closed her eyes, and rubbed them with her right hand. Sobbing sounds. No tears.

"Take your time," he said.

She covered her face with her hand. "Gail was the mum that I didn't have, because my mum passed away four years ago, and Gail's never been anything but good and kind to me." Still sobbing. Still no visible tears. "And Ian and Heather were some of the best people I've ever met. They have never done anything wrong to me, and I'm so devastated by what's happened."

She raised her left hand to her eye, wiped, then looked at her hand. "And the loss to the community. And the families. And to my own children, who've lost their grandmother." Head shaking. Bottom lip quivering.

"Can you tell us a bit more about the lunch?"

A sniffle. A couple of audible sobs. The same gesture – wiping, checking. "What I can tell you is… I just can't fathom what has happened." She shook her head slowly. "I just can't fathom what has happened. That Ian and Heather have lost their lives, and Gail has lost her life. And Don is still in hospital. And I pray…" A sob. "I pray that he pulls through. Because my children love him."

Cucchiara offered her a soft prompt. "And you must be pretty shaken up by this as well."

Erin looked up at the sky and gasped. "I'm devastated. I loved them, and I can't believe this has happened, and I'm so sorry… that they have lost their lives." Another pause. She looked at the ground. "I just can't believe it." She screwed her face up and began sobbing loudly, both hands pressed to her eyes. "I just can't believe it." She rubbed her eyes and looked at her hands again.

The front door was fifteen metres away. Between her and it stood the media. She dusted her hands together. Sniffed. Looked right, then left.

"Can you tell us where the mushrooms came from?"

She didn't answer. Instead, she turned sharply to her left, sobbing loudly, and walked all the way around her car. She stopped, briefly opened then closed the front passenger door, before continuing around to the back door on the driver's side. The media waited. She retrieved a Woolworths shopping bag of groceries from the car.

"Were they picked from the property, Erin?"

"I'm just asking you to leave me alone now, please."

"Sure," Cucchiara said. Then, "Police say you're a suspect. Do you have anything to say about that?"

She stopped.

For the first time, she looked directly at the reporter. Her voice firmed. "Yes. I say I didn't do anything. I loved them, and I'm devastated that they're gone. And I hope" — a sob — "with every fibre of my being that Don pulls through. That's what I have to say."

With that, she pulled out her keys and marched toward the front door. Shopping bag in her left hand, keys in her right. She didn't look back.

"Where did the mushrooms come from? Were they picked by you? Where did they come from, Erin? Will you tell us?"

She didn't break stride. She stepped up onto the deck, past the leaves that had accumulated in the corner of the verandah, over the skewed front doormat, and unlocked the front door.

"What meal did you cook them?"

She stepped inside.

"Did you eat the same meal, Erin?"

The door closed. The lock clicked. She was gone.

Throughout the interview, Erin had spoken of her father-in-law, Don, the beloved grandfather of her children, as still in hospital, still fighting. She had prayed, out loud and on camera, for his recovery. Don had been dead since Saturday. It was Ian who was critical. She had gotten their names wrong.

That same day, Erin emailed her sister-in-law Tanya. If anything happened to her, she wrote, she would be grateful if the children could stay with her and her husband Matt.

17 MEDIA FRENZY

THE STORY HAD STARTED to dominate the news cycle, both locally and internationally — *The New York Times*, *The Washington Post*, CNN, BBC, Al Jazeera. Everyone was talking about the raid on the lunch cook's home, the police interview, and the police declaration that Erin was a suspect. And the media were reporting something about a dehydrator — police had recovered one from a rubbish tip and were apparently testing it for fingerprints.

Armchair detectives had sprung into action online. TikTok and Instagram accounts dedicated solely to the case appeared overnight. YouTube channels sprouted, their hosts offering a frame-by-frame analysis of Erin's interview. Her body language. The lack of tears.

Footage of Simon, unsmiling, getting into his car and driving away from his home. Erin's house from the street. Police gathering CCTV footage from local businesses. Psychologists offering profiles. Mycologists explaining exactly what death cap mushrooms are and what they do to the human body. There was even a Nine News reporter filing a story from inside one of the garbage sheds at the Koonwarra tip, gesturing dramatically toward a skip bin behind her.

On Tuesday morning, 8 August, Erin went out. By the time she returned home, the media pack outside her gate had grown. More vans. More cameras. More microphones. More journalists, waiting.

As soon as she opened the gate, the media swarmed in.

She wasn't as accommodating as she had been the day before. Wearing a red windcheater, pants, and her usual sandals and socks, crossbody bag in hand, she raised her arm to shield her face the moment she got out of the car. She moved quickly toward the front door.

"I said all I had to say yesterday. What has happened is devastating and I am grieving too — and you guys don't have any respect for that."

"We do, but we just need to try to understand more."

She pushed through the throng. Cameras, microphones, and reporters blocked her path.

"Can I get to my front door please?"

"Obviously, you can."

"Well, then stop standing in front of me!"

"Have you had any further contact with police today?"

"Erin, we just want to know what you told the police."

As Erin reached the front door and pushed it open, her Labrador shot out into the media pack, tail wagging, looking for a pat.

Erin turned, brushing hair from her face. "You don't have any right to be on my private property or to harass me. This kind of behaviour will send someone to drive right off a bridge."

The dog was jumping on reporters.

She clicked her fingers impatiently. "Come inside. Come inside." Erin stepped out just far enough to grab him by the collar and pull him back. He trotted obediently through the door.

As she moved to close it, a reporter called out, "Erin. How are you going? Are you okay?"

"I am going shithouse! Thanks for asking. And you guys aren't helping."

The door slammed shut.

But the questions hadn't stopped. They never stopped. Where did the mushrooms come from? What had she told police in that interview?

Ten minutes later she came back out with a suitcase. She put it in the back of her car, then drove away without a word. The dramatic exit didn't last long though. She returned home the next day. She had the dog, the lambs, and the kids — she couldn't just leave.

She stayed indoors in the days that followed.

18 ERIN LAWYERS UP

ERIN'S SILENCE offered her no shelter. The media coverage was, by now, relentless.

An ABC article noted that Erin had displayed no symptoms of illness. A BBC piece was more pointed, declaring, "Oddly, Erin is fine." Reports about Simon's prior unexplained illnesses were gaining traction. It was widely reported that police were testing a dehydrator found at a local tip to determine whether it was connected to the lunch. In her police interview, Erin had denied ever owning one. She knew what fingerprints would show. It was only a matter of time.

Erin had had enough. At 9:40 a.m. Friday 10 August, she came out of the house, got into her red MG SUV, paused at the gate and, through her car window announced to the assembled media that she was "going to Melbourne to see a lawyer." With that she locked the electronic gate behind her, leaving a number of the media contingent stranded in her yard.

By the end of the day she had hired Bill Doogue,

founder of Doogue + George Defence Lawyers and one of Melbourne's most experienced criminal defence solicitors.

That evening, her solicitor's office sent police a five-page written statement on Erin's behalf. She wanted to correct the record — to address what she described as inaccuracies from her police interview the prior weekend. She said the purpose of the statement was to clear up the record because, "I have become extremely stressed and overwhelmed by the deaths of my loved ones."

She admitted she had lied to police in her interview. She blamed Simon.

Her account was this: While the children were in hospital for observation, Simon had visited. During a conversation, the subject of her dehydrator came up. She claimed that, as soon as the children left the room, Simon asked whether it was what she had used to poison his parents. Simon, in his court testimony, would deny that this conversation ever happened.

In her statement, Erin said that Simon's accusation, along with the involvement of child protection, had frightened her. She had panicked. So she lied. The dehydrator found at the tip was hers. She had thrown it out and lied about it — but only because she was stressed and feared she might lose the children.

She then turned to herself. She claimed that the relentless media attention was taking a toll on her mental and physical health.

Then she moved to the meal. She had used "mushrooms that I bought from the local supermarket as well as other dried mushrooms that I had bought from an Asian grocery store." Her lunch guests had chosen their own plates. She had simply taken the last one left.

She acknowledged that the meal had caused her guests' illnesses, but maintained it was a terrible accident. "I am now devastated to think that these mushrooms may have contributed to the illness suffered by my loved ones. I really want to repeat that I had absolutely no reason to hurt these people whom I loved."

She confirmed the children hadn't attended the lunch — they had gone to the movies. She had fed them beef Wellington leftovers the following night, with the mushrooms scraped off. Of her own hospitalisation, she wrote she had presented with stomach pains and diarrhoea, been placed on a drip, and given what she was told was a liver-protective drug.

Several media outlets inaccurately reported that Erin's written statement to police had been prompted by Erin giving a 'no comment' police interview the previous weekend.

Within days, the contents of Erin's statement were splashed across newspapers and news broadcasts, with multiple outlets claiming to exclusively reveal the details. Erin denied sharing it with the media. "I didn't put any statement out," she said. "I have no idea how it got out. I made a statement to the police." A police spokesperson described the leak as unhelpful to the investigation.

A 'No Trespass' notice appeared on Erin's front gate. A laminated piece of paper prominently titled "Legal Notice" forbade media from entering her property "as marked by the boundary fence."

On Tuesday 29 August, she visited her lawyer at his

Queen Street offices in Melbourne. Somehow the media got wind of this, and there was a large group waiting for her when she exited the building with Doogue. Erin looked unimpressed. She wore the same fixed expression she would carry for much of what followed. The media clamoured around her. She said nothing.

19 SEE YOU LATER

DON AND GAIL'S funerals were a private family affair, but a public memorial was held at 2 p.m. on Thursday 31 August at the Korumburra Indoor Recreation Centre. The media came. Camped outside, with cameras rolling as mourners arrived. It was an unwelcome but inevitable intrusion.

Over 400 people came to pay their respects. Every chair in the auditorium was taken. Latecomers stood along the back and side walls. The room was quiet in the way large gatherings sometimes are when no one knows quite what to say.

At the invitation of the Patterson family, Reverend Fran Grimes, Minister of the Anglican Church in Korumburra, led the service. Ian, Gail and Don's pastor, was still in hospital.

The service included memories, prayers, and hymns.

Don's brother, Colin, reflected on the couple's younger years, how they met, stories of their lives together, and the fact that they had been married for 50 wonderful years. A montage of photos played on a large screen behind him.

Simon was next. Reading from prepared notes, and with a tissue in his hand, he paid tribute to his parents as family-oriented, generous, and open-minded about people of different faiths and cultures. He shared anecdotes of a trip with Don. He said the fact that they died on consecutive days "reflected the togetherness they had worked so hard to achieve." He became emotional, telling the audience that his mother's last text in the family chat group was, "Lots of love to you all." In finishing, quietly crying, he said, "In their dying days, as they lay in hospital in comas, it was comforting to know that when we said 'see you later,' we knew it was true. The only thing that we didn't know was when. In the meantime, we'll miss them."

Simon's brother, Matt, read tributes from people overseas — from China, Botswana, and the UK — reflecting Don and Gail's years of missionary and community work abroad.

Emotional, pre-recorded audio tributes were shared by Don and Gail's grandchildren. As the children spoke, another photo montage played. "Nanna used to read with me, and I loved cooking with her. Her orange cake was my favourite," said one. Another remembered Gail's delicious homemade mayonnaise. Their tributes brought many mourners to tears.

There were further speakers. School representatives. Church and community leaders.

In the days following the memorial, the family arranged for a recording of the service to be shared via the Korumburra Community Noticeboard on Facebook, so that those who couldn't attend could still be part of it. It was a thoughtful gesture.

Erin did not attend the funerals or the memorial.

Heather's memorial was delayed so Ian could attend. He had spent five weeks in intensive care and a further two in rehabilitation before being discharged on Friday 22 September. Against all odds, one of Erin's lunch guests had survived.

The service, to "Celebrate the Life of Mrs Heather Alison Wilkinson," was held at the Korumburra Indoor Recreation Centre at 11 a.m. on Wednesday 4 October. The same venue as Don and Gail's. The order of service featured a photo of Heather on her wedding day 44 years earlier.

In advance, the family asked that, instead of flowers, donations be made to the Austin Hospital, or through SIM Australia to the Galmi Hospital in Niger, West Africa — a cause close to Heather's heart.

On the day of Heather's memorial it rained. Just as it had on the day of Don and Gail's.

As more than 400 people filed in from the wet, the opening notes of James Taylor's 'You've Got a Friend' filled the room. It had been one of Heather's favourite songs. Ian walked in with the aid of a walking frame.

Those who loved her took turns to speak. A childhood friend who had known Heather since kindergarten. Her son, David. Former colleagues. Her grandchildren, who fondly remembered her cooking, her sewing, her creativity, her laugh — and the fact that there was never a dull moment in her company.

A former principal of Korumburra Secondary College

spoke of her quiet, tireless work with students who had struggled. She had dedicated many years to helping others. She was still doing so right up to her death, via volunteer work at Milpara Community House.

"Heather led a life of service," said Dr Graham Toohill, "caring for others with a very gracious heart."

Hymns were sung. Prayers offered.

Afterwards, Ian stayed at the door for more than half an hour, hugging people, talking with them, thanking them. A man still finding his feet, giving what he had to the people who had loved his wife.

Again, Erin was absent.

ACT III — THE NET TIGHTENS

20 THE MUSHROOMS

AUTUMN IN VICTORIA marks the beginning of mushroom season. As the weather cools and dampens, mushrooms proliferate. For recreational foragers, this means walking paddocks in search of button mushrooms, or heading into pine forests for varieties like saffron milk caps, slippery jacks and jills. It is a popular pastime, but not a casual one. Mushroom foraging requires precise identification skills. Many edible species have dangerous, sometimes deadly, look-alikes, and proper identification means checking every feature — gills, stem, smell, and habitat — not just colour.

In May 2024, a 98-year-old Melbourne woman cooked a meal for herself and her son using mushrooms she had found growing in her front garden. Both became severely ill. She died a week later from multi-organ failure. Her son survived. Coroner Judge John Cain confirmed the mushrooms were death caps.

The Victorian Poisons Information Centre, operating out of the Austin Hospital in Melbourne, receives between

300 and 400 enquiries about mushrooms every year. It is unsurprising, then, that the Victorian Department of Health reinforces these dangers via seasonal awareness campaigns and warnings against foraging wild mushrooms. Their campaigns include strongly worded cautions that, unless you are an expert, you are far safer sticking to mushrooms purchased from supermarkets or greengrocers.

Of the poisonous varieties in Australia, the yellow-staining mushroom is the one most often misidentified and therefore consumed. Commonly found in gardens and lawns, it is sometimes mistaken for a common field mushroom. When eaten, it typically causes severe gastrointestinal symptoms but is rarely fatal.

The death cap mushroom, belonging to the *Amanita* genus, is found on every continent except Antarctica. In Australia, it is most common in cooler regions such as the Australian Capital Territory and Victoria. Typically found at the base of oak trees, the death cap has a smooth cap that ranges from yellowish green to olive brown, often with a faint greenish hue. The gills are white, as is the stem, which carries a soft white ring or skirt partway down. At the base, close to ground level, sits a distinctive round cup-like bulb — the feature that most distinguishes it from edible varieties. Young death caps are rounded and dome-shaped, close enough to a button mushroom to mislead the unwary, but they flatten and spread as they mature, reaching up to fifteen centimetres across, though many remain much smaller, closer to five.

Death cap mushrooms contain a group of toxins known collectively as amatoxins. The most lethal of these are two specific compounds — alpha-amanitin and beta-amanitin — the toxins forensic scientists test for when death cap poisoning is suspected. These mushrooms are incredibly toxic — half a death cap contains enough poison to kill an adult. And amatoxin is extraordinarily stable. Soaking, cooking, or drying does nothing to diminish its toxicity. Once ingested, it attacks liver cells at the molecular level. Silently. For hours after ingestion — sometimes twelve hours or more — there are no symptoms at all. Then comes what appears to be food poisoning — vomiting, diarrhoea, severe cramps. Then, cruelly, symptoms ease. The patient starts to feel a bit better. All the while, the liver is failing. By the time the third phase arrives — jaundice, organ failure, the body in full collapse — the window for intervention has often already closed.

The toxins pass through the bloodstream quickly. By the time a patient is sick enough to present to hospital, blood tests will often return a negative result. And while urine testing offers a longer window, it is only reliable for a few days after ingestion. But amatoxins leave a signature that cannot be erased. The damage they inflict on the liver is catastrophic and distinctive — a pattern of soaring liver enzymes and acute hepatic failure that experienced clinicians recognise.

It was not a specific toxicology screen that first identified the poison in this case. It was the destruction that the toxin left behind. Dr Beth Morgan, the overnight registrar at Dandenong Hospital, ordered liver function tests on Don during the night and found the results so grossly abnormal that routine food poisoning could not explain what she was seeing. His AST level — an enzyme primarily found in the liver — was 583. Normal is between 5 and 40.

All four lunch guests were tested for amatoxins between 25 and 32 hours after the lunch. Toxicology samples from Don and Ian came back positive for death cap toxins. Samples from Gail and Heather did not — not because they hadn't been poisoned, but because only blood samples were taken, and the toxin had already cleared their bloodstream.

Erin and the children were tested later. No toxins were found in their systems.

The question then was, where had the death caps come from?

Death caps only grow in the wild. They are not commercially cultivated as they have no commercial application. No food producer grows them. No supply chain carries them. Mushrooms sold in supermarkets and shops are produced under strictly controlled conditions — conditions that make it impossible for a toxic variety to accidentally enter the supply chain. This is why the Victorian Department of Health did not immediately issue a recall against Woolworths when Erin claimed she had purchased her mushrooms there. Had there been any credible risk of contamination in the commercial supply chain, a recall would have followed. But the investigation concluded that the death caps did not come from any commercial source. They could only have been foraged.

But Erin had been steadfast. She had never foraged. She had bought the fresh mushrooms from Woolworths, and the dried mushrooms from an unidentified Asian grocer — purchased, she said, back in April. She had told the doctors this. She had told the police this. She had told the Department of Health this. If that were true though, there would have been three months of contaminated stock sitting on a shelf in an Asian grocery store somewhere. There would have been other poisonings. There had been none.

Death caps do not end up inside a beef Wellington by accident. They cannot be ordered, purchased, or stumbled upon in a supermarket. To get death caps into a meal, someone has to go and find them — in the wild — harvest them, and prepare them for cooking. That takes knowledge, intention and time. And it leaves a trail.

By early August police were already looking.

21 BEFORE ANYONE IS WATCHING

THE HOMICIDE SQUAD opened an investigation on Thursday 3 August 2023. Five days after the lunch. No one had died yet — but it was inevitable. Their early involvement wasn't an indicator of suspected foul play. It was a smart acknowledgement that, if foul play was involved, time was of the essence.

Homicide investigations are complex and resource-intensive. They require experienced investigators, systematic evidence collection, and an immediate, meticulous approach. Delay is the enemy. Memories fade. CCTV gets overwritten. Evidence disappears — or, more ominously, is destroyed.

Police work from the inside out. They start with those closest to the event and work their way outward, eliminating people as evidence rules them out or alibis are confirmed.

In this case, Erin was the starting point. That made sense. She was the lunch host. She had cooked the meal.

She had been released from hospital on 1 August — unlike her guests, who were, by then, in intensive care.

The following day, 2 August, Erin was busy. At 11:09 a.m. she factory reset one of her mobile phones, then drove to the Koonwarra Transfer Station to dispose of something in the e-waste skip bin. She paid the $13.50 tip fee with her credit card, creating a digital footprint. She was not a stupid woman, but this was a stupid mistake. On the same day she had the health department hassling her. Calling. Texting. Erin was ignoring their calls. Monash Council was searching Asian grocery stores. They were trying to pin Erin down on specifics to help the search. She was expecting Cripps from Child Protection at her home at 1:00 p.m. She had a lot going on. The digital trail, it appears, had slipped her mind.

By the time the Homicide Squad started their investigation the following day, Erin was home. Her guests were still alive.

Detective Leading Senior Constable Stephen Eppingstall of the Homicide Squad was appointed Informant. In Victorian police practice, Informant is the designation for the officer appointed to lead a homicide investigation. It is not a colloquial term. It is a formal role — the detective who owns the case from the first evidence request to the last day in court. From the Homicide Squad's headquarters at the Victoria Police Centre in Spencer Street, Melbourne — a two-hour drive from Leongatha — Eppingstall began methodically. As he later explained under cross-examination, "I want everything. I'm greedy, I'm the Informant, I want everything I can get, but I don't get everything all the time."

Eppingstall and his team got to work. Bank records, supermarket loyalty card data, phone carrier data, medical records. None of it was visible to Erin. But all of it pulled her into sharper focus.

By Friday morning, the team had found two recent transactions of interest. Both at the Koonwarra Transfer Station — the local rubbish tip. The first was on 29 July, the day of the lunch itself. The second was four days later, on 2 August.

A call was made to the Koonwarra Transfer Station. Operations Manager Darren Canty retrieved the CCTV footage and relayed what he saw to the police. The same woman and the same red car appeared on both dates. On 29 July she disposed of cardboard and some other rubbish. On 2 August, she had thrown a large black electrical device in one of the skip bins. Canty was asked to have one of his team members retrieve it. The black device was a Sunbeam Foodlab dehydrator.

Eppingstall came immediately. The media captured footage of him at the tip. Dark jacket, police lanyard, a thick file under his arm.

He inspected and photographed the dehydrator. The impact of landing in the skip bin had done some damage — the front door had fallen off, the trays were in disarray, and the casing split on one side. But otherwise, it looked new. Dark paint. No fading.

He knew who had dumped it. The credit card transaction matched. The car in the footage matched. Now he needed to understand why.

He carefully packed it to take it back to Melbourne for forensic analysis.

22 THE SMOKING GUN

BY THE TIME Eppingstall returned to police headquarters in Melbourne, it was early Friday evening. He immediately sat down and watched the CCTV footage. In one video, a red MG pulled up outside a green shed. A heavy-set woman got out. She was wearing a grey, baggy jumper, white pants, sandals and white socks. He was looking at Erin Patterson. The video then showed her going to the back of her vehicle, retrieving the black appliance, leaving the vehicle's rear hatch open, and carrying the appliance into the waste shed. On her return to the car, she gave a quick glance to her left, closed the hatch, and left. She was out of her vehicle for less than a minute. She left the tip just after 11:30 a.m.

The Sunbeam Food Lab dehydrator is a squat, square appliance with six drying trays and a clear viewing door. Sunbeam promotes its ability to dry apricots, vegetables, and more.

During their search of Erin's bank records, Eppingstall's team found a credit card transaction for the purchase of a Sunbeam Food Lab DT6000 dehydrator at Hartley Wells Betta Home Living in Leongatha. At 12:17 p.m. on 28 April 2023, Erin had paid $229 for it.

The dehydrator she had dumped at the tip was less than four months old. It was hers, it was new, and she had lied about it. The instruction manual was still sitting in the bottom drawer of her kitchen. And Erin hadn't just owned the dehydrator. She had talked about it, posted photographs of it online, and shown it off to friends. The police would find those posts. But not yet.

The dehydrator itself was forensically examined. Seven samples of vegetable matter and debris were scraped from inside the trays and sent for testing. Fingerprints were lifted from the device.

A print on the rear of the device matched Erin's left hand. The debris came back positive for *Amanita phalloides*. Death cap mushrooms.

The object she had driven to the tip and tossed into an e-waste bin had her fingerprints on it, and it contained traces of the same toxin that had just killed three people and left a fourth fighting for his life.

23 THE WRONG PHONE

ERIN HAD KEPT the same mobile phone number since 2021. It ended in 783. That was the number Simon had for her, the number on her hospital admission records at Leongatha, the number she provided to the health department, and the number Dr Webster gave police when he called triple zero.

Her SIM card, which held that number, was inside a Samsung Galaxy A70 handset, in a pink flip case. Hospital CCTV from 31 July, after she returned to the emergency department, shows a pink cased phone sitting among her personal belongings.

Carrier records showed the 783 number had been heavily used in the months leading up to the lunch — hundreds of calls and over a thousand text messages. In court, it was referred to as Phone A. Phone A was active before and during the police search of Erin's home, but shortly after midday that day, it dropped off the network.

Investigators quickly established that the phone Erin had handed Farrell at the dining table during the police search — the Samsung in an orange flip case, the one that didn't need a PIN — was not her regular phone. This phone had a SIM ending in 835. The SIM had only been activated on 11 July 2023 — eighteen days before the lunch. They were able to establish that, until 3 August it was actually inside one of Erin's Samsung tablets, used for data.

Investigators also determined that on Thursday, 3 August, the same day Erin deleted herself from the family Signal chats, someone had removed the 835 SIM from a Samsung tablet and placed it into Erin's spare Galaxy A23.

During the police raid three days later, the 835 SIM was used to make calls for the first time since Erin had purchased it. Three calls to be exact — all on 5 August, all during the brief window when Erin was given privacy to contact her lawyer. The prosecution would later allege that was the same window of time where Erin had removed the 783 SIM from Phone A and secreted it from the search team. Alone, behind a closed door.

At the end of the search, when Farrell asked for her phone, Erin handed him what investigators would later refer to as Phone B. In her recorded interview at Wonthaggi later that afternoon, she gave detectives the Phone B number — ending in 835 — as her own.

Carrier records later confirmed that Erin's usual SIM, the 783 number, had been used after 6 August, but that it was no longer in her Samsung Galaxy A70. Rather, it was now in a second Nokia handset. This one was referred to in court as Phone C.

The 783 SIM remained active in Phone C for nine days, until 14 August, when it disappeared from the network entirely. Neither Phone A nor Phone C was ever found.

Then there were the factory resets.

Modern forensic techniques are highly sophisticated. After Phone B was retrieved from the police locker and examined, forensics specialists established that it had been factory reset four times — once in February and three times in August.

The first reset was on 12 February 2023. The second was on 2 August 2023 at 11:09 a.m. — performed just minutes before Erin was captured on CCTV at the Koonwarra Transfer Station disposing of a dehydrator. Her lunch guests were by then fighting for their lives in the Austin Hospital.

The third was on 5 August at 1:20 p.m. — during the police search of her home.

The fourth was at 5:16 a.m. on 6 August — the morning after the police raid.

And even though the phone had been reset multiple times, and much of its content had been destroyed, the resets themselves became evidence. The forensic analysis could pinpoint exactly when each one had occurred — and the timing told its own story.

24 WHAT THE DEVICES REMEMBERED

SHAMEN FOX-HENRY, a Senior Digital Forensic Officer with the Victoria Police Cybercrime Squad, was tasked with examining and extracting digital evidence from the electronic devices seized from Erin's home.

He used a program called Magnet Axiom, a specialist digital forensics platform used by law enforcement to recover, analyse, and report on evidence from computers, smartphones, cloud services, and other devices.

Magnet Axiom's power lies in its consolidation capabilities. Using it, Fox-Henry could extract forensic copies of the data from every seized device — the Cooler Master PC, a black Scorptec gaming computer, Phone B, and Erin's Samsung tablets — then load them all into a single file, alongside data pulled from Erin's cloud accounts. The software then merged and indexed everything, presenting what it found in a searchable visual interface — browser history, cached files, downloaded documents, chat logs, cloud-stored photographs. It could recover deleted files, map relationships between activity across devices and the cloud, and trace digital breadcrumbs that a manual search would never find.

With the combined dataset assembled, Fox-Henry ran keyword searches across everything at once. He looked for terms like "death cap," "death cap mushroom," "mushrooms," and "poison." This process produced what he referred to as Extraction Records: outputs that identified the existence of certain files with pointers that traced each hit back to the device it came from.

Many of the search results were not documents. Rather, they were brief strings of text — fragments stored in application cache, a form of temporary memory where the operating system logs traces of activity. The strings were readable lists of characters representing paths that had existed on the device at the time the cache was created. They could show that a user had accessed certain content — but they could also, in some cases, have been generated by automatic processes.

The Scorptec gaming computer yielded several of these cached strings. They referenced death cap mushrooms, poison hemlock, the iNaturalist website, and an article about the fungi of Melbourne written by mycologist Dr Tom May, which included photographs of death caps growing under oak trees in the Royal Botanic Gardens. The strings were time-stamped across a date range from late 2021 to mid-2023. They indicated that this material had been present on the device, though their nature made it difficult to definitively establish that the device user had deliberately sought out that particular content. What they did show though, was that references to death cap mushrooms and other poisons had touched Erin's home computer — repeatedly, and over an extended time period.

Phone B — the one Erin had handed to police in early August — also gave up evidence. Fox-Henry's analysis could pinpoint exactly when the factory resets had occurred, and he was also able to retrieve a number of historical data remnants. Despite Erin's efforts, not all the data had been destroyed.

But it was the Cooler Master PC — the old computer police had found stashed in the back of Ben's wardrobe — that gave the prosecution a compelling digital sequence. At 7:20 p.m. on 28 May 2022, a Bing search was made for the term "iNaturalist." The browser then navigated to inaturalist.org and to its world map of death cap mushroom sightings. By 7:23 p.m. the user had clicked through to a specific local sighting — death cap mushrooms at Bricker Reserve in Moorabbin, posted just ten days earlier.

Fox-Henry confirmed the page had a visit count of two — it had been looked at more than once. Less than a minute later, the same computer was used to search for "Korumburra middle pub" and order a family pack of food, delivered to Erin's then-address in Korumburra. The order included her name and her phone number. The prosecution relied on this sequence — a targeted search for local death cap sightings followed immediately by a takeaway order in Erin's name — as proof that Erin herself had been the one sitting at the keyboard.

From one of the Samsung tablets, Fox-Henry recovered two PDF documents relating to poisons. One was an appendix from a 2007 textbook on criminal poisoning, downloaded on or before 12 October 2019, and another on red kidney bean poisonings in the UK, downloaded on or before 27 October 2020. The tablet also contained photographs of mushrooms taken in 2020, and a search history for "stage 4 cancer," "ovarian cancer," and "brain lymphoma." The cancer searches would become more meaningful once investigators confirmed Erin had never been diagnosed with cancer.

The tablet also held a series of photographs, recovered from the cache of the Google Photos app, showing mushrooms laid out on the trays of a Sunbeam Food Lab Dehydrator, being weighed on kitchen scales. The metadata showed the photos were taken between 30 April and 4 May 2023. Erin had purchased her dehydrator on 28 April. The prosecution would later argue she had been weighing them to calculate a fatal dose.

There was one more device. During the August raid, police found a black Samsung phone in the wardrobe of an upstairs bedroom. It hadn't been wiped or factory reset. Erin probably hadn't used the handset in months — but it was still logged into her old Facebook account under the name "ErinErinErin." Although she had closed that account a couple of days before the raid, Facebook does not delete user accounts immediately. They keep them in a 30-day grace period in case the user changes their mind and wishes to re-activate the account. In Erin's case, that delay meant her data could still be accessed.

Every Messenger conversation she'd had on her other devices had quietly synced across to the black Samsung in the top of the wardrobe. It gave police a trove of chats, including the messages to and from the private group that had become her closest social circle, the small splinter group of women she had bonded with through the Keli Lane forums.

Among them were the hostile messages about Simon and his parents that she had shared with her online friends in late 2022. The bitter rants about the child support dispute. The contempt for Don's advice that she and Simon should pray together. Police read every message, and every reply. They painted a picture of a woman whose private feelings toward the people she had invited to lunch differed greatly from the warmth she projected in person.

The devices had given up a great deal — death cap searches, mushroom photographs, documents about poisons, dehydrator images, cancer research for a diagnosis that didn't exist, and private contempt for her in-laws. They formed a damning digital trail that, despite Erin's efforts with factory resets, SIM swaps and missing phones, she had been unable to fully erase.

25 INATURALIST

INATURALIST IS a website that enables members of the public to record, identify, and map observations of plants, animals, and fungi. It is used to track species distributions, assist in scientific research, and document nature through photos. In the context of death cap mushrooms, it is used by both researchers and the public to track the location of death cap mushrooms, usually so that they can be avoided, not harvested.

Erin was familiar with the website. Her home computer had been used to perform searches on it as early as May 2022.

In the autumn of 2023, there had been a number of death cap mushroom sightings not far from her home. Very specific details, including the exact locations, had been shared on iNaturalist.

Christine McKenzie, a retired pharmacist, had been visiting her daughter in the regional township of Loch. It was mid-April, and the oak trees at Memorial Reserve were putting on a stunning autumn display. McKenzie went for a walk with her husband, grandson, and their dog through the reserve, close to the picturesque suspension bridge. On the western side of the football oval, she noticed death cap mushrooms growing under an oak tree. Prior to her retirement, McKenzie had spent seventeen years as a Senior Poisons Information Specialist at the Victorian Poisons Information Centre. She knew exactly what she was looking at. The reserve had a picnic area and a children's playground — she was worried about the risk of an unsuspecting child or dog coming into contact with them. So she pulled all the death caps out of the ground, photographed them, and placed them into a dog poop bag for disposal. She had her daughter post a warning on the Loch community Facebook page.

On 18 April, under the username 'chrismck', McKenzie posted four photographs of the death caps with the Memorial Reserve location geo-tagged to the iNaturalist website. The post was publicly accessible to anyone browsing the site.

Four weeks later, Dr Tom May, Principal Research Scientist in Mycology at the Royal Botanic Gardens Victoria, was in Outtrim to give a presentation to a local community group about fungi. On the afternoon of 21 May, he went for a walk and found death cap mushrooms growing in Neilson Street. He was unsurprised. It was autumn, they were near an oak tree, and the soil was reasonably moist after recent rain. At 2:50 p.m. that day, under the username 'funkeytom', he posted a couple of photos, including one of a large death cap, with a smaller one sitting to its left, along with the location to iNaturalist. Like McKenzie's post, it was publicly accessible. The geo-tagged location was within roughly 20 metres of where he had found them.

Two publicly accessible posts pinpointing death cap locations in Erin's local area — posted just months before she served a meal that contained them. Investigators already had photographs from Erin's tablet showing mushrooms consistent with death caps being dehydrated in her kitchen in late April 2023. She had to have sourced them somewhere. But no browser history on any of her seized devices placed her on iNaturalist in April or May 2023. Investigators had no evidence of Erin undertaking searches that may have led her to McKenzie's post in Loch, or May's in Outtrim. They suspected she had used Phone A — her primary phone throughout those critical months — the missing phone.

26 WHERE THE PHONE HAD BEEN

THE DIGITAL FORENSIC evidence had established what Erin's devices contained. Cell tower analysis would attempt to establish where the missing one had been.

For this, the prosecution engaged Dr Matthew Sorell, a digital forensics and telecommunications specialist from Digital Forensic Sciences Australia. His role was to map the movements of Erin's main phone in the months leading up to the fatal lunch. Crucially, this did not require the physical handset — Sorell could use data provided by Erin's carrier.

The principle behind the analysis is straightforward. A mobile phone, when switched on, connects to nearby telecommunications towers. Each connection is logged by the carrier. By mapping which towers a phone connects to, and when, an analyst can estimate the phone's approximate location at any given time. Cell tower data can suggest where a phone may have been, but it cannot confirm it definitively.

Sorell was given data covering the period from 2019 to

2023. There were two types of records made available to him. Call charge records provided basic details — calls, texts and data usage. Event-based monitoring records were far more detailed, capturing the constant signalling between a phone and the network — potentially five to ten records per minute, compared with one every fifteen minutes for call charge records. Event-based monitoring is costly and time-consuming, so investigators had only obtained this data for a limited set of specific dates of interest, selected on the basis of what the call charge records initially revealed.

Beyond tracking where Erin's phone had been, Sorell could use the carrier data to identify which physical handset her SIM was in at any given time. Every mobile phone carries a unique identifier — an IMEI, or International Mobile Equipment Identity — which is logged by the carrier alongside SIM card activity. This enabled investigators to reconstruct the movement of Erin's SIM card between handsets.

From June 2021 to January 2023, Erin's primary SIM, ending in 783, was in an older Samsung Galaxy. On 15 January 2023, it moved into Phone B, a Samsung Galaxy A23. Then on 12 February 2023, it moved into Phone A, a Samsung Galaxy A70. This was significant because Phone A, with the 783 SIM, had been Erin's primary phone throughout the period in which prosecutors alleged she had been searching for death cap mushrooms. Because they never recovered the phone, investigators were also denied the opportunity to examine its internet search history — including any potential searches for content on iNaturalist.

The 12 February 2023 handset change was helpful for investigators though, as it meant that from that date forward, Sorell was able to track the unique handset identifier – the IMEI number - for the Samsung A70, connecting to towers. He could be confident it was the same physical device throughout all of the critical months.

Sorell's analysis was presented in four reports, each one built around the phone's movements on dates of particular interest. The first analysed possible visits by Erin's phone to Outtrim. The second concerned trips coinciding with the episodes in which Simon had fallen ill — times relevant to the attempted murder charges that would ultimately be severed from the trial. The third examined possible visits to Loch, and the fourth included event-based monitoring and detailed tables for Outtrim on 22 May 2023.

From Erin's home in Leongatha to the suspension bridge on Loch-Poowong Road in Loch — where McKenzie had photographed death cap mushrooms — was a drive of around 25 minutes. Leongatha to Neilson Street in Outtrim — where May had found and photographed death caps — was about 18 minutes. Similar travel times, but in different directions.

Both towns fell within Erin's regular driving range. She travelled these roads routinely. The South Gippsland Highway connects Leongatha to Loch, and the Bass Highway connects Leongatha and Inverloch, passing near Outtrim. This proximity was important. It meant that her phone connecting to towers near Loch or Outtrim was not, on its own, remarkable. The question was whether the pattern of connections on specific dates suggested something more than routine travel.

Sorell's language throughout his reports reflected caution. He spoke in careful terms: possible, not confirmed. He could not speak of a visit to a specific address. He could not exclude the possibility that the phone had been outside his defined areas on any of the dates in question. He acknowledged that Erin regularly travelled roads passing through or near both Loch and Outtrim, and that routine travel could account for some of the tower connections. He accepted that weather, topography, and antenna tilt could all affect which tower a phone connected to and, that in some circumstances, a phone could connect to a tower as far as 60 kilometres away. These were not weaknesses in Sorell's work. They were the honest parameters of what cell tower data can and cannot do.

With clear parameters established, three dates stood out.

McKenzie had posted her death cap sighting at Loch to iNaturalist on 18 April 2023. Ten days later, on the morning of 28 April, Sorell's analysis showed a pattern consistent with Erin's phone visiting the Loch area between 9:06 a.m. and 10:07 a.m. The event-based monitoring records showed the phone connecting to cell towers at Loch or Loch South at 9:08 a.m., 9:09 a.m., and 10:01 a.m.

At 12:17 p.m. that same day, Erin visited Hartley Wells Betta Home Living in Leongatha and purchased the Sunbeam Food Lab Dehydrator.

Investigators drew the two threads together. A possible

visit to a known death cap site in the morning. The purchase of a device capable of preserving mushrooms that afternoon.

The second date of interest was 22 May 2023. Dr May had posted his death cap sighting at Outtrim to iNaturalist on the afternoon of 21 May — the day before.

Sorell's analysis showed Erin's phone connecting to towers in Loch on the morning of 22 May, between 9:19 a.m. and 10:02 a.m. — the phone connecting to the Loch South cell tower about every five minutes, consistent with it remaining relatively stationary. Later that same morning, the phone was on the move, now connecting to towers in the Outtrim area. Both locations were where death cap mushrooms had recently been photographed and reported on iNaturalist.

Sorell's work had further limitations. For the purposes of his analysis, he defined "Outtrim" as the entire Outtrim postcode area, as mapped by Google Maps. This area is larger than the small township of Outtrim itself — and certainly much larger than Neilson Street, where May had found the mushrooms. A possible visit to the Outtrim postcode area was not the same as a possible visit to Neilson Street.

This was also an instance where different levels of data told different stories. The initial call charge records had suggested Erin's phone may have merely passed through the Outtrim area — consistent with routine travel along the Bass Highway. But when Sorell undertook analysis of the more detailed event-based monitoring data for that date, the picture changed. The more granular data indicated her phone had lingered in the area, consistent with a stop rather than a drive-through.

Then there was 31 July. The 90-minute window between Erin leaving Leongatha Hospital at 8:10 a.m. and returning at 9:48 a.m. had already raised questions. This was the morning that she had been told that her guests had likely consumed death cap mushrooms. In her interview, she had told Eppingstall that she had to go home. The cell tower data contradicted this.

Between 8:55 a.m. and 8:58 a.m. that morning, Erin's phone connected to towers in the Outtrim area. Not towers her phone would ordinarily connect to from her Leongatha home, but in the opposite direction — toward Outtrim via the Bass Highway. There was then a gap in the records before her phone reappeared on Leongatha towers at 9:23 a.m.

Where she went during that window, and why, was never established. What the data did establish was that Erin's account — went home, fed the animals, packed a ballet bag, and had a lie down — did not match where her phone had been.

The data had placed Erin's phone near known death cap sites on two occasions — 28 April and 22 May 2023. Both dates corresponded with iNaturalist posts made shortly before. One was the same day Erin purchased the dehydrator. On the third occasion — 31 July — the phone had connected to towers in the Outtrim area during a period she claimed to have been at home.

The phone evidence alone was not damning, but it was another piece in a puzzle that investigators were steadily assembling.

27 THE PUZZLE COMES TOGETHER

ERIN'S electronic devices had given up their secrets. The cell towers had traced her phone's movements. Elsewhere, other streams of the investigation were delivering results of their own.

In late August, toxicology testing was completed on the beef Wellington leftovers that police had retrieved from Erin's bin on 31 July, the morning she presented at Leongatha Hospital. The results confirmed the presence of beta-amanitin in samples of the mushroom paste and the beef.

The meal Erin served her guests had contained death cap mushroom toxin.

Forensic testing of seven samples scraped from the dehydrator trays had also confirmed, with 99 per cent accuracy, the presence of death cap mushroom residue. Four of the seven samples tested positive for alpha- and beta-amanitin.

Police also had the CCTV footage of Erin carrying the

dehydrator into the tip, and her fingerprints on its casing. Death cap residue in the trays. Her hands on the machine. And a video of her throwing it away.

Eppingstall's team confirmed that Erin's claim of having cancer was a lie. This one was easy. Under Victoria's Improving Cancer Outcomes Act 2014, every hospital, pathology service, and health provider in the state — public and private — is required by law to report cancer diagnoses to the Victorian Cancer Registry. The Registry is operated by Cancer Council Victoria and functions as the central repository of cancer data for the Victorian Department of Health. If Erin had been diagnosed with cancer, a record would exist. There was no record.

Investigators had also, by now, subpoenaed Erin's medical files and had them examined by intensive care specialist Professor Andrew Bersten. There was no appointment for an MRI. There was no appointment for a needle biopsy. In her text messages with Gail, she had claimed to have undergone these procedures in June 2023. There was no evidence of a cancer diagnosis, and no evidence that she required a biopsy at all. The medical crisis that had assembled her victims at the table was now provably false.

Bersten's review didn't stop there. He also examined Erin's medical records from her hospitalisation after the lunch. His conclusion: There was no evidence she had suffered any acute illness on 30 July, and no evidence of liver injury. Her lunch guests had been in intensive care with catastrophic organ failure. Erin had been mildly dehydrated at worst.

Police had checked the Woolworths supply chain. They confirmed two farms supplied the Leongatha Woolworths — Costa Group in Mernda and The Mushroom Place in Reservoir. Investigators visited both facilities and filmed their production processes. They categorically ruled out contamination from the commercial supply chain.

But Woolworths had more to offer the investigation than clean mushrooms.

Investigators had subpoenaed Erin's Everyday Rewards loyalty card data. It revealed a peculiar pattern of purchases in the days leading up to the lunch. On Sunday 23 July, six days before she had hosted the lunch, Erin purchased sliced mushrooms, puff pastry, filo pastry, and shallot onions. On Thursday 27 July, two days before the lunch, she was back — more pastry, more sliced mushrooms, and beef fillets. On Friday 28 July, the day before the lunch, she returned a third time. Yet more pastry. Yet more mushrooms. More beef. Along with Gravox granules, frozen mashed potatoes, and beans. Three trips to the same supermarket in six days — each time, buying the same core ingredients for the same meal.

The case was far from complete. But it was strong. They had the messages. The phone substitution. The phone movements — Loch in April, Outtrim in May. The factory resets. The dehydrator purchase. Her prints on it. The poison inside it. CCTV of her throwing it away. The fake cancer diagnosis and other lies. The forensic results. Death cap toxin in the food and in the victims. And on 19 September — three days before he was released from rehabilitation at Heidelberg — they had a statement from the sole surviving lunch guest, Ian Wilkinson. They had enough.

Erin was still free. Going about her daily life. But that was about to change.

28 THE SECOND KNOCK

POLICE ARRIVED at Erin's home at 8:00 a.m. on Thursday 2 November 2023. They were there to execute their second search warrant at 84 Gibson Street, Leongatha. Erin was arrested shortly after. It had been 96 days since she had hosted the fatal lunch.

They knew Erin had lied to them, and that she had not given them her main phone — Phone A. They knew from Erin's phone records it had been her primary device from 2021 to just after the first raid. They had its IMEI number. They knew that, on the day Erin self-presented at hospital, she had it with her — in a pink phone case.

THIS TIME they came well prepared.

The Australian Federal Police had loaned them two specialist technology detector dogs — Alma and Georgia — Labradors trained to find electronic devices by detecting the scent of the components inside mobile phones, laptops, and similar devices. Alma was flown down from Queensland for the search. Georgia was already deployed in Victoria.

The search team was fastidious. With the aid of Alma and Georgia, they searched Erin's house, yard, car, and garage. They even searched the overstuffed old couch on the balcony outside the dining room where she had hosted the lunch.

Over six hours, police carried a series of sealed evidence bags out to their vehicles.

The search yielded items that had not been located in the first raid. Between them, the dogs found a mobile phone, five tablet devices, a trail camera used for outdoor motion-activated photography, a USB stick, and two secure digital (SD) cards. They also found an empty box for a Samsung Galaxy A70 handset. Police believed this was the box for Phone A, but they found no trace of the phone itself.

Five weeks earlier, on 24 September, Erin had come out of her home and thrown unidentified rubbish into a large yellow skip bin in her front yard. The media was still outside her fence. One yelled out asking if they could speak to her. She yelled back, "No! Go away!" That skip bin was now gone. Police never established what, if anything, of probative value it held.

While the search was still in progress, a police press conference was held in Melbourne.

Homicide Squad Detective Inspector Dean Thomas stood at the lectern for the second time in this matter. Same dark suit, same checked shirt and same diagonally striped tie. Reading from prepared notes again, he confirmed the arrest of a Victorian woman, describing it as "just the next step" in a complex investigation that was "not yet over." He reminded the assembled media that three people had lost their lives. People much beloved in their communities and greatly missed by their loved ones. He noted the investigation had been subject to a level of public scrutiny he could not recall in any other case, nationally or internationally. This time he took no questions. He closed his folder and walked away from the lectern.

Later that day police — and the dogs — completed their search of Erin's home. Once they were done, Erin, wearing a baggy grey jumper, was taken from the house and placed in the back of a grey unmarked police vehicle.

The drive to Wonthaggi Police Station took her past the same towns she had driven through a hundred times. Arriving at the station shortly after 2:30 p.m. that afternoon, they passed through the same electronic gates into the same car park at the back of the building. The same route as her first interview. This time was different though. She was not here voluntarily. She could not just get up and leave when she'd had enough.

Erin's lawyer, Bill Doogue, met her at the station. Police interviewed her in his presence before three charges of murder and five charges of attempted murder were laid. The murder charges related to the deaths of Don, Gail and Heather. One charge of attempted murder related to Ian. One related to Simon, who was also invited to the lunch, and the remaining three charges of attempted murder related to the illnesses Simon had experienced in 2021 and 2022.

Erin Trudi Patterson was remanded in custody pending her first court appearance the following morning.

ACT IV — THE LEGAL RECKONING

29 FIRST APPEARANCE

ON FRIDAY 3 NOVEMBER 2023, Erin made her first court appearance at the Latrobe Valley Magistrates' Court.

In Victoria, the first court appearance for a serious indictable charge is known as a filing hearing. It is held in the Magistrates' Court and marks the formal beginning of the committal process — a series of preliminary hearings in the lower court to determine whether there is enough evidence to send a case to trial.

At the filing hearing, the court sets a timetable for the exchange of evidence between prosecution and defence, and fixes a date for the committal mention — an administrative hearing to confirm the evidence has been served and to decide how the case will proceed. Although murder charges commence in the Magistrates' Court, if sent to trial, they must ultimately be heard in the Supreme Court. The lower court acts as a necessary gateway — the first step in a long process.

There was a small media contingent outside the courthouse. Inside, they also filled three of the available rows in the gallery.

Flanked by two custody officers, Erin appeared wearing a beige jumper and a pair of reading glasses perched on her nose. Her face was expressionless.

The hearing itself was quite brief. Magistrate Tim Walsh presided. Her solicitor, Bill Doogue, appeared on Erin's behalf. Acting Sergeant Greg Ellis appeared for the prosecution.

The charges laid by police the previous day were read aloud — three counts of murder and five counts of attempted murder. Erin was not asked to enter a plea. At this stage of the process, she wasn't required to. That would come later.

Walsh was patient with her, taking the time to explain that the matters they were discussing were administrative, and that the main thing was for them to "progress through the system as fast as possible."

Erin nodded to indicate her understanding. "Okay," she replied.

Doogue did not apply for bail. Walsh explained to Erin that, even if he had, the Magistrates' Court has no power to grant it. Only the Supreme Court can hear a bail application for murder charges. And even then, under Victoria's Bail Act 1977, the defence must prove that exceptional circumstances exist to justify release. It is a test that is rarely met.

The next issue seemed simple enough — where and when the case would next be heard.

Both defence and prosecution sought to have the next

hearing moved to Melbourne, but Walsh was having none of it. He kept it at Morwell.

As to the matter of when, Ellis requested a 20-week adjournment. Police needed time to analyse the electronic devices they had seized during the search of Erin's home the previous day. Walsh looked annoyed. He questioned why they needed twenty weeks if they were confident enough to lay charges only the day before.

Doogue, for Erin, agreed to the delay — but used the moment to make a point: Not only was the analysis the prosecution relying on incomplete, but it hadn't been shared with the defence either. "That's why they're asking for extra time," he said.

Erin was remanded in custody, her matter adjourned to 7 May 2024 for committal mention. She was granted leave to appear via video link from Dame Phyllis Frost Centre — the women's prison that would become her home until the charges against her were decided one way or another.

30 THE COMMITTAL

IT WAS ALMOST six months before the case returned to court. Doogue remained Erin's instructing solicitor, but had now briefed Senior Counsel (SC) Colin Mandy to lead the defence in court. In the Australian legal system, solicitors and barristers perform related but different roles. Solicitors prepare the case, barristers argue it in court. In a murder trial, engaging an experienced Senior Counsel to lead is standard practice.

Mandy was a formidable choice. Appointed Senior Counsel in 2018, he was, at the time of the committal hearings, Vice-President of the Victorian Bar and Chair of Parnell's Barristers. His career had spanned murder trials in Perth, drug trials in Sydney, fraud and other white-collar matters, coronial inquests, and appeals in almost every jurisdiction in Australia. In November 2023 — just months before he appeared for Erin — he had successfully defended a Melbourne man against terrorism charges before a Supreme Court jury. If Erin intended to fight, she had hired someone who knew exactly how to.

At Erin's previous hearing, her matter had been adjourned to 7 May, but the court brought it forward to 22 April for case management purposes. This was the second time Erin had appeared before Magistrate Tim Walsh in the Latrobe Valley Magistrates' Court in Morwell. This time she appeared by video link from the Dame Phyllis Frost Centre. She was wearing a blue prison uniform and a matching zip-up jumper.

Walsh arrived at the bench at 10 a.m. and greeted Erin on screen. There was some initial confusion — her legal representatives appeared to have joined the video link for the wrong courtroom. Walsh briefly adjourned while the issue was sorted out.

Once court recommenced, the first of many pre-trial skirmishes between prosecution and defence played out over a question that might have seemed mundane to anyone watching from the public gallery — where should the committal hearing itself be held?

Mandy, appearing for the first time on Erin's behalf, indicated that Erin wanted the committal heard locally, in Morwell. It was standard practice, he argued, for proceedings to be conducted as close as possible to where the alleged offences took place — in this case, Erin's home in Leongatha, roughly sixty kilometres from Morwell. The prosecution countered that the committal could be better accommodated in Melbourne and should proceed without delay.

Walsh was caught between principle and pragmatism. He had reviewed the brief over the weekend and, describing it as "quite voluminous," he estimated the committal would require three to four weeks. The Latrobe

Valley Magistrates' Court was stretched to capacity. Consequently, he would be unable to schedule the hearing until sometime in 2025. At the same time, Mandy had another matter booked during August and September. All of this meant that Erin would have to remain in custody for at least fourteen or fifteen months from the date of charge, a prospect that weighed on the court.

Walsh floated two alternatives: moving the case to Melbourne Magistrates' Court, or fast-tracking it to the Supreme Court. Mandy rejected both. There were "powerful reasons," he said, for the committal to take place in Erin's local community, and she was content to wait. Walsh pointed out that Morwell was not actually Erin's home. Mandy countered that it was close enough "in the context of regional Victoria."

At Erin's first appearance, back in November, Walsh had kept the case at Morwell over the objections of both the defence and prosecution. They both wanted it heard in Melbourne. Now, five months later, the positions had reversed. It was the defence insisting on Morwell and, for practical reasons, Walsh trying to move the case to Melbourne. It was a small but telling reversal — and it raised the question of why Erin suddenly wanted her case heard regionally.

Walsh reserved his decision on where the committal would be held until the next hearing on 7 May. He further ordered the parties to submit their list of proposed witnesses before that date.

When the case returned to court in May, things took yet another unexpected turn.

Rather than waiting for the magistrate to share his

ruling on the location for the committal hearing, Erin's legal team elected to bypass committal altogether. Erin would fast-track her case directly to the Supreme Court.

It was a significant decision. A committal hearing would have allowed the defence to cross-examine prosecution witnesses and test the strength of the Crown's case for the first time. By electing to go directly to trial, Erin's legal team sacrificed that opportunity. But fast-tracking meant an earlier trial — and if Erin's defence was successful, she would walk free sooner.

Whether the choice was driven by a strategic assessment of the evidence, a desire to avoid the publicity of a committal, or simply a wish to move the process along was never explained in court. But the entire Morwell-versus-Melbourne debate that had dominated the previous hearing had, within the space of a fortnight, become entirely academic.

Magistrate Walsh formally cautioned Erin about the implications of entering her pleas, then offered her the opportunity to respond to each charge individually.

He read the first aloud. That at Heidelberg on 4 August 2023 she did murder Heather Wilkinson.

"Guilty or not guilty?"

"Not guilty, Your Honour."

The murder of Gail Patterson.

"Not guilty, Your Honour."

The murder of Donald Patterson.

"Not guilty, Your Honour."

Then the five counts of attempted murder. The same words, the same even tone, five more times. Eight charges. Eight denials. Her voice never wavered.

One count of attempted murder related to Ian, the sole surviving lunch guest. The remaining four all related to Simon — three for the poisoning episodes in 2021 and 2022, and one for the July 2023 lunch itself.

The three historic charges were made public for the first time. The prosecution said the attempts — the same incidents Simon had described to his family in the Austin Hospital chapel — had occurred at Korumburra on 16–17 November 2021, at Howqua in the Victorian High Country on 25–27 May 2022, and at Wilsons Promontory on 6 September 2022. The fourth Simon charge related to the lunch. It didn't matter that he hadn't attended. The prosecution's case was that, if he had, Erin intended to poison him.

For a media pack that had been subsisting on procedural hearings for months, the new charges were a windfall. Headlines were rewritten, bulletins reshuffled, and the case surged back to the front page.

The case was listed for a post-committal directions hearing in the Supreme Court on 23 May.

31 THE SUPREME COURT

THE SUPREME COURT phase began in Melbourne.

On 23 May 2024, Erin appeared by video link from the Dame Phyllis Frost Centre for a brief hearing before Judicial Registrar Tim Freeman. On the screen, she watched the proceedings impassively, her hair down, still wearing blue prison-issued clothing. There was no jury to consider, no impression to manage. That would come later, when every detail of her appearance would be carefully curated. For now, she was just another remand prisoner on a video link.

Most of what was discussed during the hearing could not be reported. The court had imposed suppression orders to protect the integrity of the proceedings and to ensure Erin received a fair trial.

The case was adjourned for three months to allow both legal teams to prepare.

But behind the scenes, a familiar tension was brewing. The battleground of geography had resurfaced.

The prosecution wanted the trial held in Melbourne,

where the Supreme Court had purpose-built facilities, ample courtroom space, and none of the logistical constraints of a regional venue. The defence wanted it held in the Latrobe Valley, as close as possible to the scene of the alleged crimes. The parties went back to court.

On 15 July, Justice Jane Dixon heard the competing arguments in the Melbourne Supreme Court. The defence relied on a well-established principle of criminal law: An accused person should be tried near where the offence allegedly occurred, where the witnesses lived, and where the community most affected by the crime was located. The prosecution argued that practical considerations — courtroom availability, security and the sheer scale of media interest — favoured Melbourne.

On 30 July, Justice Dixon delivered her ruling. The trial would be in Morwell. It was a win for the defence.

With the venue settled, the machinery of trial preparation began to grind forward.

On 21 August 2024, Erin appeared by video link for a series of pre-trial hearings before Judicial Registrar Freeman. The trial commencement date was set down for 28 April 2025 — in the Supreme Court sitting at the Latrobe Valley Law Courts in Morwell.

The pre-trial hearings continued through the week, concluding on 28 August after five days of proceedings. They dealt with contested questions about what evidence would be admissible and how the charges should be tried — but almost nothing could be reported.

For a case that had generated international headlines and daily media coverage, the contrast was stark —

months of intense public interest met by court-imposed silence.

Erin was remanded in custody until the case returned on 14 October for the second block of pre-trial hearings. These focused on witness lists and finalising which pieces of evidence would be contested in a *voir dire* scheduled for February 2025 — essentially a trial within a trial, held without the jury present, in which a judge rules on whether specific evidence is admissible. It was an important phase. What the jury would ultimately be permitted to hear depended on it.

32 THE EVIDENCE WARS

THE CASE HAD, by now, been assigned to Justice Christopher Beale. Appointed to the Supreme Court in 2014 after nearly three decades in criminal law — as a Legal Aid duty lawyer, a barrister, and a Crown Prosecutor — Beale was one of the most experienced criminal trial judges on the bench.

The February pre-trial hearings, held over seven sitting days before Beale, were the most consequential proceedings since Erin's arrest. They would shape the trial more fundamentally than anything that had come before.

At their core was a series of arguments about admissibility — what evidence the prosecution could put before a jury, and what would be excluded. Justice Beale heard submissions on seven distinct issues, each with the potential to strengthen or weaken the Crown's case.

The first issue concerned computer records seized from Erin's home. The prosecution sought to admit evidence showing that, in the period leading up to and during the alleged offences, Erin had accessed — or possibly accessed

— information online about poisons generally, and death cap mushrooms in particular. This evidence, the Crown argued, demonstrated "a continuous state of mind": a sustained and specific interest in the very substances alleged to have caused the deaths. The defence countered that much of this evidence amounted to little more than fragments — brief strings of text buried in application caches, not documents Erin had necessarily chosen to read. They argued the material was too ambiguous to prove anything and too prejudicial to be fair. Justice Beale let it in. It meant the jury would see a digital trail stretching back years — searches for death caps, visits to iNaturalist, articles about poisoning — woven through the devices found in Erin's home.

The second ruling addressed cell tower evidence. The prosecution relied on the expert analysis of standard call charge records spanning several years, as well as more detailed event-based monitoring data for specific dates. The prosecution contended that this data placed Erin's phone near the towns of Loch and Outtrim on specific dates in April and May 2023 — dates shortly after death cap mushroom sightings had been posted to iNaturalist. Both towns were within easy driving distance of Erin's home. In at least one instance, the more granular event-based monitoring shifted the picture. The call charge records suggested Erin's phone had merely passed through Outtrim on 22 May 2023, whilst the event-based monitoring indicated that it had been relatively stationary in the area. Passing through a town on a highway is unremarkable. Stopping in one is not.

The inference the prosecution invited was stark: Erin

had seen the iNaturalist posts and driven to the locations to collect the mushrooms she would later serve in the fatal lunch. The defence argued the data proved nothing of the sort. Erin regularly drove roads passing through or near both towns, and Dr Sorell's own language acknowledged the limitations — he spoke of possible visits, not confirmed ones.

Beale admitted the evidence. He found it was of modest probative value, rising no higher than evidence of opportunity. But it did place Erin within reach of death cap mushrooms at a time proximate to the lunch, and he was satisfied the evidence's limitations were clearly articulated and easily understood. It didn't necessarily prove that Erin had been there, but the jury would be entitled to weigh it alongside everything else.

The third ruling dealt with tendency evidence. The prosecution wanted to establish that Erin had a pattern — or tendency — of accessing websites about poisons and death cap mushrooms. They intended to use that pattern to support a specific inference — that she had accessed the iNaturalist posts about death cap sightings in Loch and Outtrim in April and May 2023. This mattered because no record of those specific searches existed on any seized device, and Erin's main phone had never been recovered. The prosecution needed another way to bridge the gap.

The defence argued the logic was circular: You cannot use a general pattern of searching to prove a specific search occurred when there is no evidence that it ever did. Beale drew the line. The tendency evidence was out. It was the prosecution's cleanest loss of the pre-trial period — and it meant they would have to rely on the cell tower data alone to place Erin near the mushroom sites.

The fourth ruling addressed sixteen pieces of alleged incriminating conduct — everything from Erin feigning illness, to disposing of the dehydrator, to the phone factory resets. Most were admitted, but one significant item was excluded. Less than an hour after her guests left, Erin had made a brief trip to the Koonwarra Transfer Station. CCTV footage showed her disposing of cardboard along with some other rubbish. Prosecutors sought to rely on this as evidence that Erin had likely disposed of items related to the lunch — possibly the plates — but Beale ruled it out. Without evidence of exactly what she had discarded, the jury would be invited to speculate. Police had established that Erin's council bins had ample room at the time, making the trip itself unusual, but unusual is not evidence. What prompted it, and what she threw away, remains unknown. The jury never heard about it.

The fifth ruling concerned hearsay evidence — and it carried a weight beyond its legal label. Don, Gail and Heather were dead. They could not take the stand, could not be cross-examined, and could not tell the jury in their own voices what happened at the lunch or in the days that followed. But they had said things to family and friends before they died. The prosecution sought to admit those statements through formal hearsay notices. Among them was Heather's puzzlement about why Erin had served herself on a different plate, and Don and Gail's account to family members that Erin had told them she had cancer. The defence objected. Hearsay is inherently unreliable, they argued — the people who made the statements could not be questioned about them, and memories of what someone said days before they died are vulnerable to error and emotion. Beale acknowledged the need for caution but ruled the evidence admissible. It meant that the victims would, in a sense, have their say after all.

The sixth ruling would prove to be the most contentious. It concerned coincidence evidence — and it went to the very architecture of the prosecution's case.

The Crown's indictment painted a picture of escalation. Erin, the prosecution alleged, had poisoned Simon on three occasions between November 2021 and September 2022, and had then poisoned four people — killing three of them — at the July 2023 lunch. The prosecution argued that the similarities across all four alleged poisoning events were so striking that they could not reasonably be explained as mere coincidence. Evidence of one set of events, they contended, should be admissible to prove the other.

The defence argued that allowing the jury to hear allegations that Erin had poisoned Simon on three previous occasions would be deeply prejudicial — that jurors would struggle to assess the lunch charges on their own merits.

Justice Beale agreed with the defence. He found that if the jury was permitted to hear all the evidence together, there was a significant risk they would misuse or overvalue the coincidence evidence — using the lunch poisoning to convict on the historic Simon charges, or vice versa, in a way that was not logically justified. The judge ordered that the indictment be severed: The three charges of attempted murder relating to Simon's earlier illnesses would be tried separately from the five charges arising from the July 2023 lunch — the three murders, the attempted murder of Ian, and the attempted murder of Simon by invitation.

It was a devastating loss for the prosecution. It meant they would have to prove each set of charges independently, without the reinforcing effect of the other. The jury would never hear Simon's account of his earlier illnesses, nor the details of Erin's conduct during his recovery — evidence that might have recast the lunch not as an isolated act, but as the final step in a malicious pattern.

On 21 March, Justice Beale delivered his seventh ruling, addressing a collection of miscellaneous contested evidence. These included Erin's interest in true crime, her attitude towards the Pattersons, cell tower data, a SIM card swap, and whether she had put her bins out on 3 August 2023.

The pre-trial process trimmed the prosecution's case in ways the public would never see. Before Beale ruled on the miscellaneous items, the prosecution voluntarily withdrew several — including evidence that Erin owned an extensive collection of true crime books and that she had deactivated her Facebook account shortly after the lunch. Of the items Beale did rule on, most were admitted — including the Facebook messages about Simon and his family, the post seeking advice about her non-existent cat eating mushrooms in the garden, and Erin's request to her sister-in-law that she care for the children "if anything happened." Erin's failure to put her bins out on 3 August was excluded.

The Facebook messages were a particular battleground.

The defence fought hard to keep them out, arguing that the jury might use Erin's private venting as proof of murderous intent when, in reality, they were nothing more than the frustrated outpourings of a woman going through a difficult time. Justice Beale disagreed. He ruled the messages were admissible — not as evidence of motive, but to counter what the prosecution expected would be a defence portrait of Erin as a woman on good terms with her in-laws. The messages painted a very different picture.

The pre-trial hearings had not gutted the Crown's case, but they had sharpened it — forcing the prosecution to go to trial with only the evidence that could survive scrutiny.

There was one defeat, however, that they were unwilling to accept. The loss on Ruling 6 — the severance of the three historic attempted murder charges relating to Simon. On 3 April 2025, less than four weeks before the trial was due to begin, the Director of Public Prosecutions took the matter to the Court of Appeal.

Three Court of Appeal justices — Emerton, Priest, and T Forrest — heard the appeal. The prosecution's argument was, in essence, that the evidence linking the two sets of charges was so compelling that its value to the case far outweighed any unfairness to the accused. The lunch poisoning, the Crown contended, should be available to prove that Simon was poisoned, and the earlier episodes should be available to prove that the lunch guests were also deliberately poisoned.

On 17 April, the Court of Appeal refused leave to appeal. Justice Beale had been correct to sever the indictment. The two groups of charges would be tried separately.

The practical consequence of this ruling would become apparent, in dramatic fashion, on the first day of trial.

33 ALL RISE

MORWELL, about 60 kilometres from Leongatha, is a regional town of 14,000 people. In autumn, its streets are lined with colour as trees slowly shed their leaves, and the Centenary Rose Garden displays its final blooms against the cooling Gippsland air. Once the engine room of Victoria's power industry, it is a quiet, working town not accustomed to the spotlight.

Morwell is the legal hub in Gippsland, and is home to the Latrobe Valley Justice Precinct — the multijurisdictional Latrobe Valley Law Courts, a police district headquarters, and a 24-hour police station. The court building is modern and imposing — constructed of precast concrete, metal, and glass. Natural light is drawn into the building through a series of light wells and oversized glazed windows. The building sits slightly at odds with the more traditional homes and shopfronts of Morwell.

The court complex, typically witness to a steady stream of minor criminal matters and civil disputes, has views of soft rolling valleys beyond the township. It is a long way from the grand and historic Supreme Court building in the heart of Melbourne's legal district.

It was Tuesday 29 April 2025. The commencement of Erin's trial had been pushed back a day for administrative reasons.

Members of the public had lined up before dawn, hoping for one of the limited seats in the public gallery. TikTok, Instagram, and true crime forums had been in overdrive for days. Dozens of journalists, from Australia and abroad, had descended on the small regional town. Morwell's motels were booked out. Its cafes were full. It would remain this way for the duration of the trial.

The case had everything to draw a crowd. Women are rarely charged with mass murder. The weapon — death cap mushrooms hidden in a home-cooked meal — was extraordinary. And the victims were quiet, God-fearing country people who didn't appear to have an enemy in the world.

Erin had been transported from Dame Phyllis Frost the previous day by prison van, a two-and-a-half-hour drive. She had spent her first night in the cells underneath the Morwell police station — cells not designed to hold prisoners for more than a night or two. It was to be the first of many weeks she would be held there overnight during the week, before being transferred back to Phyllis Frost at the end of the sitting day on Friday.

It had been Erin's own legal team who successfully argued that the trial should be held in Morwell — so that she might be judged by a jury of her peers. Country people. People who knew the area, understood rural life, and might see her differently than a Melbourne jury would. They won that argument. But the weekly commute and the police station cells were the price.

Erin's trial would be held in Courtroom Four, a compact room with light wood panelling. The dock was at the back of the courtroom. In Australian criminal trials — unlike the American system, where the accused sits beside their lawyers — the defendant sits separately in the dock, a convention inherited from the English courts. Erin sat there, flanked by a pair of prison officers, with her own small screen fixed in place so she could follow whatever evidence would be shown to the jury. Larger screens at the front of the room would display exhibits and video evidence.

Only six seats were allocated to media — in the back row, directly in front of the dock, assigned by weekly ballot. Reporters who won a seat found themselves sitting less than two metres from Erin. To catch a glimpse of her demeanour or reactions as the trial progressed, they would have to swivel around and face her. When they did, Erin would glare directly back at them.

For the dozens of journalists who missed out, the court offered alternatives. An overflow room on the same level as Courtroom Four — normally the jury pool room — became the nerve centre for most of the media covering the trial. Chargers snaked across tables, laptops were open, and food was eaten between updates. A large screen on the wall gave journalists a closer look at exhibits — photographs, text messages, phone records — than they would have had in the courtroom itself. It was still a court environment, but the atmosphere was slightly more relaxed. On a typical day, fifteen or so journalists worked from the room. By the time Erin took the stand, that number doubled, with BBC correspondents and other international media joining the pack. A similar setup was made available in Melbourne, and there was also a remote audio-only link available to members of the media.

Members of the Patterson and Wilkinson families were allocated seating by court staff. The balance went to the curious members of the public and true crime enthusiasts who had queued early to get a seat.

Wearing a pink and white striped long-sleeve shirt, Erin took her seat in the dock at the back of the court. Within minutes, she broke down in tears. A friend consoled her.

Dr Nanette Rogers SC sat at the bar table, closest to the jury box. Beside her were her junior counsel, Crown Prosecutors Jane Warren and Sarah Lenthall. Rogers appeared unassuming, but behind this quiet exterior was a sharp and experienced litigator. She holds a doctorate in philosophy and has built an extensive career, including more than a decade as a Crown Prosecutor in the Northern Territory prior to her appointment as a Senior Crown Prosecutor in the Victorian Office of Public Prosecutions in 2013. Both Warren and Lenthall were accomplished advocates in their own right.

Rogers had arrived that morning in a practical jacket and scarf, backpack on her back. For criminal trials in regional locations like Morwell, the court often dispenses with formal robing and wigs to create a less intimidating atmosphere for the jury and local witnesses. Rogers leaned into that informality: no gown, no bar jacket, just professional dress and the quiet confidence of someone who knows how to command the room.

Across the bar table sat Colin Mandy SC, the experienced Senior Counsel who had already appeared at Erin's pre-trial hearings, alongside his junior, Sophie Stafford, and instructing solicitor Bill Doogue. Stafford was an accomplished junior with a growing reputation. Together, they formed a well-balanced and deeply experienced defence team. Mandy and Stafford had chosen the traditional formality of the bar — wearing the black gowns and bar jackets of their profession. Absolutely appropriate, but in visible contrast with the prosecution team.

Photography is prohibited inside Australian courtrooms, so the media had no opportunity to take photos of Erin in court. At an earlier hearing, Erin's legal team had also secured a ban on media publishing any image showing her as a prisoner — arguing that such images might prejudice her right to a fair trial. In practice, this meant images of her court arrivals and departures were unusable, since she always arrived handcuffed and flanked by guards.

With no photos of Erin available, court sketch artists filled the void. One sketch from the first day of trial was used widely in print media — Erin in her pink and white striped shirt, looking bulky, dour, and heavily shadowed, her hair loose, her neck prominent. There were other sketches as the weeks went on. None were particularly flattering.

A knock from the judge's chambers. There was a sense of tension and anticipation in the courtroom.

"All Rise."

Justice Christopher Beale entered. The Supreme Court was now in session. In Morwell.

Before the court turned to its first order of business, Erin's barrister raised Erin's conditions with the judge. Her cell was cold. She had no quilt or pillow. She had been given a blanket but had "spent the night cold — and awake because she was cold — and she can't operate like that." He requested that she be given writing implements, a computer and a charger, arguing she required "special treatment so that we can do our job properly, so that she can provide us with proper instructions. So that she's not uncomfortable." Victoria Police pushed back, citing security concerns and pointing out that Erin's legal team had been told as far back as June 2024 that she would not have access to a computer in the cells. A compromise was reached. She would be given a laptop — but not a charger.

With Erin's dissatisfaction regarding her conditions partially resolved, Beale turned his attention to jury selection.

In the months before the trial, court authorities had sent jury service notices to thousands of potential jurors drawn from the Gippsland community. Through a process of questionnaires, random ballot, and self-exclusion, the pool had been whittled down to 120 potential jurors — known as the jury panel.

It is normal practice for the jury panel to sit in the trial courtroom to receive information and directions from the judge. However, given the large size of the jury panel in this case, and the small size of Courtroom Four, potential jurors — now referred to by numbers rather than names — were spread across three rooms: the trial courtroom, another courtroom on the same level, and the jury panel room. The rooms were connected to a video conference feed from Courtroom Four so those in the other rooms could see and hear Beale.

Beale took the jury panel through the matter and shared a list of potential witnesses, places, and legal practitioners who would be involved. He gave panel members an opportunity to excuse themselves if they knew someone from the list, or if they didn't think they could be impartial. That left 85 in the pool.

Of those, a court associate pulled numbers from a box and announced each number along with the person's job title. If they were not already in the trial courtroom, the person would come in and take a seat in the jury box. The prosecution and defence were both allowed up to three peremptory challenges. That is, the right to reject a prospective juror without giving a reason. Through her lawyers, Erin used all three. The prosecution didn't stand aside any of the jury panel.

The process took over half of the first sitting day, but ultimately whittled the panel down to 15 jurors — ten men and five women. This was a jury of twelve with three alternates. Beale had added the three alternates to ensure the trial wouldn't be derailed by illness or other misadventure. This would later prove particularly prudent.

As the newly empanelled jury settled into their seats in the jury box, Beale delivered a bombshell. Erin would not be facing any attempted murder charges relating to Simon. He told the jury to put those charges out of their minds.

The severance ruling, upheld by the Court of Appeal on 17 April, had required the three historic poisoning charges to be tried separately. Rather than run that separate trial, the prosecution discontinued them. But they also chose to discontinue the fourth Simon charge — his attempted murder by invitation to the lunch itself — even though the severance had not required them to. That charge could have proceeded alongside the other lunch charges. Why the prosecution elected to drop it was never publicly explained.

Beale moved to jury instructions. He told the jury that Erin didn't have to prove her innocence. She didn't have to prove anything. It was up to the prosecution to prove the charges that had been brought against her.

He warned the jurors not to conduct their own research. They were not to discuss the case on Facebook, Twitter, or blogs. They were to avoid social media. Each juror was given a court-issued iPad to enable them to view exhibits close up. Beale said they were to decide the case on the facts, "using your head, not your heart." He then told them that, once they were sent out for deliberation, they would be sequestered — staying in a motel in a controlled environment, designed to reduce their exposure to outside influences.

Day one was over. Fifteen jurors went home knowing they would be back in the morning.

Outside the courthouse, journalists scrambled for position — recording pieces to camera, feeding the podcasts, and filing stories. The dropping of the Simon charges had given them their first substantial headline for months. After the long road to trial, Erin Patterson was back in the news. Tomorrow, the courtroom would hear what the prosecution said she had done.

34 OPENING STATEMENTS

THE SECOND DAY of the trial, Wednesday 30 April 2025, was cool. Autumn leaves swirled around and gathered in doorways as the courthouse came to life. Rogers and Eppingstall arrived together. They were early. She had her backpack on her back, a handbag in one hand, and a trolley of files in the other. She was ready.

Despite the chilly weather, the crowds were also back. A long queue of members of the public snaked outside the courthouse, all hoping for a seat. Many had travelled long distances. Many would come back again and again, every day of the trial.

Once the court complex opened, just over twenty members of the public filed into Courtroom Four to take up seats in the public gallery. Ian, along with members of his extended family, settled into their reserved seats.

Erin was brought up from the Morwell cells. Wearing a blue striped shirt, she took her seat in the dock. Detective Inspector Dean Thomas, the man who had fronted the media conferences, head of the homicide squad, watched from the public gallery.

Once the jury was brought in, and the judge entered, proceedings commenced.

Beale started by taking the jurors through a checklist: the elements of murder and attempted murder. The prosecution would need to prove four things: Erin had caused the death of her guests by serving them a poisoned meal, her conduct was "conscious, voluntary and deliberate," she intended to kill or cause really serious injury, and she had done so without lawful justification or excuse.

The floor was now Rogers'. The prosecution's opening statement was substantial.

She set the scene for the jury, meticulously leading them through a detailed background. She discussed Erin and Simon's history, the conflict between them the prior year, the lunch held four weeks before the fatal one, then the circumstances of the lunch itself — including Simon's refusal to attend on either occasion. She laid out what would become the scaffolding of the prosecution's case: that Erin had fabricated a cancer diagnosis to draw her guests to her home, deliberately sourced and prepared death cap mushrooms, faked illness after the lunch to avoid suspicion, and destroyed and concealed evidence.

Rogers then moved into the details. She pointed to Erin's Facebook messages, her increasing animosity toward Simon and his parents, the different plates Erin had served her guests on, the individual portions of beef Wellington, and the elaborate cancer lie that had drawn the guests to her table. She went through the symptoms Erin's guests had suffered and told the jury that Erin had faked illness afterwards, which explained her reluctance to be treated at hospital. She described how Erin had lied when she said she had fed the children leftovers from the meal. Death cap toxins had been found in the remnants of what she said she fed them, yet the children never became unwell. She also detailed Erin's shifting stories about the source of the mushrooms — Woolworths in Leongatha, an Asian grocer in Clayton, Oakleigh, Mount Waverley. Wherever. Rogers set out the tip visit and the SIM swap. The phone resets.

She took the jury to posts Erin had made in an online group chat, where she had written about dehydrating mushrooms, blitzing them into powder, and hiding them in food without her children knowing.

She explained that the prosecution would show the jury extensive evidence to prove their case, including oral evidence from a variety of expert witnesses, photos, diagrams, maps, and statements. There would be cell tower data suggesting Erin had visited areas where death caps were found in the months prior to the lunch, along with the phone evidence and dehydrator evidence — including CCTV footage of Erin disposing of it at the Koonwarra tip.

Rogers had essentially provided a snapshot of the architecture of the prosecution case. She also made one thing clear: The prosecution did not intend to try to prove a motive. They didn't need one. They just needed to prove criminal intent. But it was hard to miss the contradiction — Rogers had just spent hours walking the jury through Erin's private resentments, her hostile messages about the Pattersons, and a relationship that was visibly fraying. She never called it a motive though. She didn't have to.

She finished by reminding the jury that the onus was on the prosecution to prove its case beyond a reasonable doubt. "But," she said, "your role is to be impartial and to make a decision at the end based on the evidence that you have heard and seen in this trial."

Rogers sat down. By the time she had finished speaking, it was after 3:30 p.m. — her opening address had taken up almost the entire court day.

Mandy then rose to give his opening statement.

He pointed out that, in contrast to the prosecution, his address would be brief. He said this was because the prosecution had to set out how their evidence would unfold. He didn't have to do that. His client didn't need to prove anything. "By contrast to that kind of address, the purpose of an opening address for the defence at this stage of the trial is limited," he said.

He reminded the jury that his client was innocent until proven guilty. "You've heard that phrase before, I'm sure," he said. "But it's not just something that people say. It's a fundamental principle, and it protects all of us. It's the law." Charges were easy to lay. "It's proving them that matters."

He told the jury that what had happened was a tragedy. A terrible accident. His client had served the meal, and she now accepted that death cap mushrooms were in it. But she had not poisoned them deliberately. After all, she had fallen ill too.

"She wasn't pretending to be sick.... The defence case is that she was sick too, just not as sick," he said.

The case, he argued, came down to a single question. "It's about what she meant to do, what she intended to do. Did she intend to kill these four people? That's the issue."

Mandy painted a picture of his client's character. Erin was a devoted mother — caring, kind and attentive. She was comfortable financially and generous with her money. He said it was not in dispute that she and Simon had separated some years earlier, but they had continued to enjoy a good friendship until a disagreement about child support arose towards the end of 2022. He told the jury that Erin's relationship with Don, Gail, and the children would be a critical issue during the trial.

He made a series of concessions. Erin had never been diagnosed with cancer. She had dumped a food dehydrator and she had lied to police about it. She had also lied about foraging for mushrooms, though she denied ever deliberately seeking out death caps. But Mandy framed the concessions carefully. He asked the jury to consider why she would lie about owning a dehydrator when her husband, her children, and her Facebook friends all knew she had one. It didn't make sense — unless, of course, she had panicked.

That was the defence's explanation for Erin's questionable behaviour in the days after the lunch. She had panicked. She was overwhelmed by the fact that four people had become gravely ill from food she had served them. It had been the reaction of a frightened woman, not a killer.

He told the jury there were a number of other issues raised in the prosecution's opening that he would not address at this stage, but he did wish to emphasise that the intention to kill or harm was "very much in dispute." He asked them to keep an open mind until they had heard all the evidence.

With that, he returned to his seat. He had spoken for less than thirty minutes.

It had been a long day for the jury, but it was over. Tomorrow, the prosecution would begin calling witnesses, and the jurors would begin the real work of deciding which account to believe.

35 THE CROWN CASE BEGINS

IT WAS THURSDAY 1 MAY, day three of the trial. Courtroom Four was full. Again. As it would be every day for the duration of the proceedings. The media, allocated their seats by ballot, were settled in their designated positions. Eager members of the public — those at the front of the daily queue outside the courthouse — had filled the remainder of the gallery.

Ian was there. He would attend most days.

At the rear of the room, Erin took her place in the dock. She wore the same pink and white striped shirt she had worn two days earlier. Her glasses pushed up onto her head, she maintained an almost disinterested gaze. Unreadable.

Up to this point, the trial had been about the architecture — directions and openings. The dry but necessary scaffolding of legal process.

Now that architecture would come to life. Brick by rhetorical brick. Over the next five weeks, Rogers would call more than fifty witnesses to build the Crown's case.

The public had followed this story for nearly two years, but suppression orders had kept most of the details out of the press. People knew the broad strokes — three dead, a dehydrator found at a tip, an accused woman who had sobbed without tears on her driveway. What they didn't know was what the forensics had found inside that dehydrator, what Erin's devices remembered, where her phone had been, or what she had written to her friends when she thought no one was watching. Rogers was about to show them. And Mandy, through cross-examination, would do everything he could to blunt each blow as it landed.

In front of Erin, the six journalists who had managed to get a seat in the court were a study of concentration. Absorbing every word and gesture, they had spent the last two days typing furiously on their laptops. They were seated about two metres behind the prosecution bar table. Nanette Rogers rose. She addressed Beale, "It is very difficult to concentrate sitting at the bar table with the clackety-clack-clack behind us." The judge smiled wryly and asked the media to be mindful of the distraction. The typing didn't stop. It just got a little quieter for a day or two.

Rogers called her first witness.

Simon Patterson.

He entered the witness box and was sworn in. He wore a dark suit, white shirt, and a purple-blue tie. He looked composed but nervous.

Rogers began by establishing the background for the jury. Through a series of measured questions, she walked Simon through his family background. His parents, Don and Gail; his aunt and uncle, Ian and Heather; the broader

Patterson and Wilkinson families. A family tree was displayed for the court. Simon shared that he had met Erin while they both worked at Monash Council, that they had married in 2007, and that their first child, Ben, had been born in Perth.

Simon told the court about Erin's inheritance from her grandmother, and about the early tensions that had slowly unravelled their marriage. He described their move back to Victoria and how, in 2015, Erin had purchased a home for them in Korumburra — in her name alone. They lived there briefly as a family, but then Erin bought a second house in Korumburra and moved into it with the children. Without Simon.

"It was always her leaving me," he said.

He looked downcast as he told the court he had always tried to maintain a good relationship with Erin, for the sake of the children. Then he paused. His words faltered. He asked for a tissue.

Rogers asked if he would like a break. He said he was okay, but that he was struggling with his answers.

She moved carefully into questions about the shift that came in late 2022. When Simon declared himself separated on his tax return.

He told Rogers he felt a substantial change in their relationship after that. Disputes over child support, arguments about school fees, increasingly hostile messages from Erin in the family Signal group. Rogers took him through it methodically. Asked to summarise their relationship at this time, he replied, "The chatty nature of it pretty much stopped."

Rogers asked what Erin's relationship with his parents

had been like previously. Simon said that she had always gotten on well with them — particularly his father. But that changed. He said that, although there were issues between him and Erin, "it was pretty clear" she was trying to draw his parents in. His parents had responded by encouraging them to sort it out between themselves. Erin wasn't happy. He had suggested mediation. "I was keen to resolve it because Erin and my parents' communication about it… it wasn't working," he told the jury. "From my point of view, Erin was being extremely aggressive, so I thought a mediator would probably help us communicate."

Then Rogers turned to the lunch.

Simon confirmed that Erin had approached him after church with the invitation. "I was a bit reluctant, but I said, 'yes. That should be okay' or something like that," he said. He'd spoken to his parents about it afterwards. None of them knew what the lunch was really about — what the medical issue was, or why Ian and Heather were also being invited. Don's best guess was something about Erin having a lump on her elbow.

Simon confirmed that, after the invitation at church, he didn't see Erin until after the lunch.

Rogers took him to the message Simon had sent Erin the night before the lunch. She displayed it, along with Erin's reply, on the courtroom's big screen. Trial Exhibit 2.

6:54 p.m. 28 July 2023. Simon to Erin:

> *Sorry I feel too uncomfortable about coming to lunch with you, Mum, Dad, Heather and Ian tomorrow, but am happy to talk about your health and implica-*

tions of that at another time if you'd like to discuss on the phone.

6:59 p.m. 28 July 2023. Erin to Simon:

That's really disappointing. I've spent many hours this week preparing lunch for tomorrow which has been exhausting in light of the issues I'm facing and spent a small fortune on beef eye fillet to make beef Wellingtons because I wanted it to be a special meal, as I may not be able to host a lunch like this again for some time. It's important to me you're all there tomorrow and that I can have the conversations I need to have. I hope you'll change your mind. Your parents and Heather and Ian are coming at 12.30."

The language in Simon's message echoed the text he had sent a month earlier, when he declined the June lunch — the same phrase, "too uncomfortable," used again.

Simon nodded. He remembered the text exchange. He expressed bewilderment at the fact that Erin said she had medical news to discuss, yet the lunch was a full two weeks after the invite. He had simply assumed it couldn't be anything too urgent.

Rogers didn't ask, and he didn't explain, the reason for his "too uncomfortable" statement. Based on pre-trial rulings, any discussion of Simon's prior illnesses — and his suspicions that Erin had tried to poison him — was off limits. At one point, when the jury was out of the room, Simon said he was "half-thinking about the things I'm not allowed to talk about," and that "the legal process has been very difficult… especially the way it's progressed in terms of the charges relating to me."

But there were things Simon could tell the jury. Important conversations that only he could share. Rogers took him to the conversations he'd had with Heather and Don in their dying days — the hearsay evidence Justice Beale had ruled admissible in the pre-trial rulings.

Simon shared that Heather had questioned why Erin served herself from a different plate to those of her guests.

He went on to describe visiting his father in hospital — visibly ill, discoloured, his voice strained. He detailed their bedside conversation — Don telling him that, at the lunch, Erin had claimed to have cancer.

He described a text Erin had sent him from Leongatha Hospital, complaining that the doctor was "being mean" to her. He confirmed that Erin had told him she had fed the children steak, mash, and beans for dinner on Sunday night — leftovers from the lunch.

Rogers sat down.

Mandy rose for cross-examination. He needed to soften the edges Rogers had sharpened — explain some things, create a little doubt on others.

He pressed Simon on his relationship with Erin. "It went up and down," Simon replied. Mandy asked Simon about his child support assessment, and about him not contributing to the school fees. Simon replied that he was advised he would be "double paying" if he paid Erin child support as well as the school fees. Mandy responded that the child support amount — $38 per month — would not even cover the school fees, much less any of the other expenses for the children. Simon agreed, and said that this had caused friction between him and Erin.

Under Mandy's questioning, Simon confirmed that Erin didn't have many plates — perhaps eight to ten, and certainly not a matching set. He recalled one colourful plate in particular. It was one that belonged to Kate.

Mandy took Simon through a couple of months of text messages between him and Erin. Arrangements around the children. Logistics of the weekly church livestream. Some minor bickering. Mandy reframed these as ordinary domestic friction. Certainly not motive.

He homed in on the messages between them in late 2022. Simon spoke of the tension between himself and Erin, and Erin and his parents. Despite Mandy's efforts to show the messages as minor tiffs, Simon characterised Erin's messages of that time as "inflammatory" and "extremely aggressive." Mandy countered that both parties' behaviour had actually been quite poor, saying, "It had descended into some pettiness, if I can put it that way, on both of your parts." Simon conceded that was probably a fair characterisation of where things had gotten to between the two of them.

Mandy revisited Simon's use of the word "aggressive." He emphasised that Erin's messages showed hurt and insecurity, not hostility. He put to Simon, "That's not the right way of categorising it, is it? She was upset, she was hurt." Simon wasn't going to have his words changed. He replied, "Perhaps you could put up the messages that she messaged the group chat that I mentioned and we can see." Simon won that round.

Mandy turned to Simon's earlier testimony that Don

had told him Erin had announced she had cancer. Mandy pointed to the circumstances. Don was in hospital. He was very ill. The conversation was short. He suggested Simon may have misunderstood, and that Don could have said a suspected diagnosis, not a confirmed one.

Simon was clearly annoyed.

"I reckon we're starting to get in the realm of flying teapots territory," he retorted.

"I'm sorry, I missed that?"

Simon doubled down, "It's possible that there's a flying teapot going around Mars, but it's pretty unlikely. Miscommunications happen. It's possible I've misunderstood everything you've said so far, and you've misunderstood me. But I don't think we probably have."

Mandy didn't react. He simply moved on.

He accused Simon of failing to keep Erin updated on his family's condition in the days after the lunch. Simon agreed that was true, but added, "It intrigued me that she never actually asked how they were."

Having tested some of the key points of Simon's evidence, Mandy then turned to building his own picture of Erin. Simon agreed that she was a devoted mother. Her daily life revolved around the kids. On the question of Erin's premature departure from hospital, Simon confirmed that she'd had a number of prior bad experiences. "Yes. Erin hates hospitals," he said.

Their friendship had been strong until late 2022. He restated his belief that Erin struggled with low self-esteem and was unhappy with her weight. He talked about their early relationship. He thought her Christian faith was sincere. He had no idea she owned a dehydrator.

Point by point, Mandy had assembled a counter-portrait. A loving, generous woman — overwhelmed, not calculating — with no reason to kill the people closest to her.

Mandy had no further questions. Simon was excused.

He had been in the witness box for the best part of three days. He was tired and emotional. His relief at being excused was palpable. In the dock at the back of the court, Erin did her best to maintain an air of disinterest in the proceedings.

Crown prosecutor Sarah Lenthall examined the three Facebook friends — Christine, Daniela, and Jenny. All were members of the smaller, breakaway group where Erin had shared her most candid thoughts. All appeared via video link. None had met Erin in person.

Their evidence overlapped considerably. All three confirmed Erin's dehydrator purchase in early 2023, her posts about blitzing mushrooms into powder and hiding them in food, and beef Wellington recipe discussions in July. The screenshots were entered into evidence: "I've been hiding powdered mushrooms in everything," and her comment about the dehydrator reducing mushroom mass by 90 per cent. None recalled Erin ever mentioning mushroom foraging. All agreed that Erin seemed to be a good mother, though Christine added that Erin "seemed unsettled whenever the kids were away."

Where their evidence diverged was in what Erin had told them about Simon. Christine testified that Erin had described him as "controlling" and "coercive," and that she felt "challenged" by his family's demands. She told the court Erin had described herself as an atheist. Daniela told the court that Erin had shared with her that Simon was "just so religious," and that he "put the church before her and their family." She went on to say that, based on what Erin had told her, she didn't think Simon was a very nice person.

But it was Jenny — a semi-retired social worker and competent cook — who gave the most detailed evidence. She had read about the deaths in the paper, and connected the dots. It was Erin's beef Wellington meal. She reached out to Erin online. Erin asked her to call instead. Their phone conversation lasted ten minutes. Erin told her the mushrooms had come from an Asian grocer. She said she was sick. She said the children had eaten some of the meal. Then Erin cut the call short — she said her lawyer was ringing. It was the last time Jenny ever spoke to her.

Mandy cross-examined each of the three briefly. He challenged their recall, explored whether they had loyalties that might colour their view of Erin, and suggested each had turned on their former friend. When he cross-examined Jenny, he asked whether beef Wellington was one of her favourite dishes. It was. It was a small moment, but it served the defence well — the beef Wellington wasn't some exotic or sinister choice. It was a dish friends discussed over chat, swapping tips the way people do.

Jenny was excused shortly after 3:25 p.m.

The jury was dismissed for the day just after 4 p.m. Simon Patterson's evidence was done. The three Facebook friends had come and gone. The prosecution had laid the groundwork — the fractured marriage, the mounting grievances, the dehydrator, the mushrooms hidden in everything.

36 THE SURVIVOR SPEAKS

IAN WILKINSON TOOK the stand on the sixth day of the trial. He was the only person, apart from Erin herself, who could share what had happened in her home at lunchtime on 29 July 2023. As he walked to the witness box, Erin's eyes briefly met his. Then she looked away. She would appear largely unmoved throughout his evidence — occasionally shifting in her chair, swivelling it slightly from side to side, but she was otherwise still and expressionless.

Crown prosecutor Jane Warren led him through his evidence. She began with his relationship with Erin. They were not close, he said. "More like acquaintances." Their relationship, "didn't have much depth." He knew her mostly through the Korumburra Baptist Church, where he was the pastor and where Erin periodically helped with the livestream.

"She just seemed like a normal person to me," he said. "When we met things were friendly. We never had arguments or disputes."

When the lunch invitation came — extended to

Heather at church two weeks earlier — the Wilkinsons were pleased. They had never been to Erin's home before.

"We were very happy to be invited," Ian told the court. "It seemed like maybe our relationship was going to improve."

The court was shown a copy of Heather's diary. She had written "Erin for lunch" in pencil. Below it, in blue ink: "12:00" — the time the Pattersons were to pick them up. And the word "fruit," for the platter she was taking.

Warren was methodical. She took Ian through the arrival, the garden tour, the pantry Erin was reluctant to show, the plating of the food. Much of it confirmed what the prosecution had already outlined in its opening. But hearing it from the man who had eaten the meal, lost his wife, and nearly died himself gave the evidence a gravity that no summary could replicate.

Ian confirmed that Erin had plated the food herself and refused offers of help. He described the beef Wellingtons as individual portions, "like a pastie," completely encased in pastry with mushrooms inside. He told the court there were four large grey plates and one smaller plate — "an orangey-tan sort of colour." Gail and Heather had each picked up two of the grey plates and carried them to the table. Erin held the smaller, differently coloured plate back, then carried it to her place at the table.

An annotated photograph of the dining table, marked with each person's position, was entered into evidence. Ian said that there was no designated seating. They sat where they liked.

He confirmed who ate what — he and Heather

finished their portions, Gail ate half of hers, Don finished his own and then ate Gail's leftovers. "There was talk about husbands helping their wives out," Ian said. He couldn't say with certainty how much Erin ate, only that she was "definitely" eating.

Then came the moment the prosecution had been building toward. The cancer announcement.

"She plainly said that she had some sort of cancer," he said. "I thought, 'this is the reason we've been invited.'"

He recounted what Erin told them. "Her voice was low at that point. I couldn't quite catch exactly what kind of cancer she was naming, but she named a type of cancer. She went on to speak about the scan and that this was a serious, serious situation. A situation that made her afraid for the future of her kids." He said she asked for their advice, "'Should I tell the kids, or not tell the kids about this threat to my life?'"

In the dock, Erin faintly shook her head.

Ian testified that Erin hadn't gone into detail about what treatments she would need. The conversation was short — perhaps ten minutes — before the children and a friend arrived back at the house.

"I realised we weren't able to continue, and that we hadn't prayed about it," Ian said. He led the group in prayer, asking for God's blessing — that Erin would get the treatment she needed, that the children would be okay, and that she would have wisdom in how she told them.

The jury already knew the cancer claim was a lie. The defence had conceded as much in its opening. But Ian hadn't known that when he prayed for Erin's health. He had taken her at her word and asked God to help her.

Warren then took Ian through the night of the lunch, the dawn phone call to the Pattersons and the discovery that they all had the same symptoms. "We all had constant vomiting and diarrhoea," he said. Ian told the court he had arranged for a church member to cover his sermon.

Ian confirmed that Simon had driven him and Heather to Leongatha Hospital, where doctors treated them for food poisoning. "My memory is that suspicion was falling on the meat," Ian said.

But the next morning they were, "abruptly woken up by a group of nurses who literally ran us down the corridor in our beds to the urgent care area." A doctor told them there had been communication indicating the symptoms were consistent with suspected mushroom poisoning. "He was very frank," Ian said. "He said it is a very serious situation. He said there was a time-critical treatment available."

The last thing Ian remembered was being given a charcoal substance to drink. There were several weeks after that he could not recall. He would spend three weeks in intensive care at the Austin Hospital, seven weeks in hospital in total. He very nearly died.

It was now Mandy's turn. After the lunch break, he began his cross-examination.

Mandy can be formidable in cross-examination, but he is also canny. Ian Wilkinson was a quietly-spoken, credible witness. Attacking him directly would risk alienating the jury. Instead, Mandy probed the reliability of Ian's recollections — his weeks in an induced coma, the extended hospitalisation, the grief of losing his wife. The implicit question was whether such an ordeal could have affected the precision of his memory.

He started gently, having Ian confirm details about Erin's church attendance, her relationship with Heather, and the conversation just prior to the group sitting down for lunch. Ian recalled that, as Erin prepared the meal, he and Don had chatted about a book they had both recently read. Heather and Gail had offered to help serve, but Erin declined. She plated the food herself.

Mandy then moved to the plates. His line of questioning sharpened slightly.

He suggested that four grey plates were not used at all. Ian disagreed. He remembered four grey plates. Mandy suggested there was no smaller plate. Ian didn't budge. "The plate was smaller, a different coloured plate," he replied. Mandy pressed on, suggesting that once the plates were placed on the bench, the guests were free to pick up whichever one they liked — that there was no deliberate assignment. But Ian's account was specific. Erin had plated the food at the bench. Gail and Heather had each picked up two of the grey plates and carried them to the table. Erin had held the odd plate back — the smaller, lighter one — and carried it to her own place. Nobody chose. Erin kept hers separate.

Ian's voice had grown increasingly strained as the afternoon wore on. But Mandy wasn't finished.

He took Ian to the interview he had given to police on 19 September 2023 — nearly two months after the lunch. In that statement, Ian had said Erin revealed she had "suspected cancer." Mandy asked whether that had been true at the time.

"I think I was probably understating things at that point," Ian replied.

"So it wasn't the truth?" Mandy pressed.

Ian didn't waver. "Erin was fairly clear that the diagnosis was given," he said.

Mandy had Ian agree that, apart from the cancer announcement, the lunch conversation was just day-to-day, family stuff.

This set the scene for one last question.

"It was just a normal lunch," he suggested.

"Yes," Ian replied.

Mandy finished his cross-examination. Ian was excused.

He stepped down from the witness box and walked slowly across the courtroom to the public gallery, where a member of the Patterson family put his arm around Ian.

In the dock, Erin's expression did not change.

Weeks later, in his closing address, Mandy would return to this thread of questions. He told the jury that witnesses could hold "imperfect and honestly mistaken memories," that Ian and others had been under enormous pressure in the days following the lunch, and that the prosecution had cherry-picked the recollections that suited its case while ignoring those that didn't. It was a careful argument — not that Ian was lying, but that even a good and honest man could remember imperfectly.

37 THE FAMILY SPEAKS

DURING THE SECOND week of the trial, members of the extended Patterson and Wilkinson families took the stand. Their raw, often tearful evidence filled in the spaces around Simon and Ian's testimony — the hospital vigils, the family dynamics, and the small details that only people close to the victims could provide. Much of what they described had already shaped the investigation. Now it was being said under oath. For the jury.

For these families, the courtroom was just another room in a building they never asked to enter. They had already endured the hospitals, the funerals, the media camped outside their homes. Now they were being asked to sit in a witness box and relive it, in front of strangers and the media, while the woman accused of killing their loved ones sat only metres away.

Anna, Don and Gail's youngest daughter, fought back tears from the moment she was sworn in. She told the court her parents had mentioned the lunch invitation over dinner two days beforehand. She found the inclusion of

Ian and Heather unusual — they had never been invited to Erin's home before.

Anna confirmed that she had travelled to Dandenong Hospital on the evening of 30 July to be with her mother. She stayed overnight. Gail was in intense pain. "I took her to the bathroom many times," she said. Through the exhaustion, Gail told Anna that when she had been vomiting earlier, there had been a strong taste of mushrooms in her mouth. Asked whether Gail had shared anything else about the lunch, Anna said her mother had told her "it went well." Under cross examination, Anna shared that Erin and Simon had lent her and her husband money to purchase a home some years prior.

Matt, Simon's brother, shared details of a call he made to Erin on the Monday after the lunch. He said that, while he was with Don in the intensive care unit, a hospital staff member had enquired where the mushrooms in the meal had come from. Matt called Erin and asked her. She nominated two sources — fresh mushrooms from Woolworths and dried mushrooms from a Chinese grocer or supermarket in the Oakleigh area. He confirmed he passed this information on to the medical staff. He also told the court that, after his parents' deaths, Erin had emailed his wife asking whether they could care for her children, as Child Protection were involved.

Under cross-examination, Matt confirmed he too had received a substantial loan from Erin and Simon and that, in 2021, Erin had organised a lunch with him in Melbourne to discuss her sadness about the state of her relationship with Simon. She had sought his advice on how to get Simon to attend counselling with her.

Ruth, Ian and Heather's youngest daughter, told the court she didn't know Erin well. She had heard about the lunch invitation during a family gathering and was confused by it — as were her parents. Erin had never invited them to her home before.

Tanya, Matt's wife, gave evidence that she had texted Erin on Monday 31 July, then visited her the next morning. Tanya said that, during their text exchange, Erin had written to say she was nauseous, dizzy, and tired.

Tanya arrived to visit just before 10 a.m. on Tuesday morning. She told the court that, shortly after her arrival, a staff member came in with Erin's blood results and told her she was fine to go home.

Tanya told the court that Erin had asked about the lunch guests, but she'd been careful in her response, saying things were "going downhill quickly," though she didn't have the latest updates. Tanya explained that she and Matt had already agreed not to share too much about their loved ones' conditions, believing it wasn't their place. They felt it was better for Simon to decide what he would tell Erin.

According to Tanya, Erin said she was aware that both Don and Gail had been placed in induced comas. At some point, the conversation shifted to lighter topics, including cruises. Tanya had recently been on one, and Erin mentioned she was thinking of taking the kids on a trip.

The children's evidence was handled differently. Neither Ben nor Kate appeared in person.

Their testimony had been recorded in police interviews conducted at the Morwell Police Station in August 2023, a couple of weeks after the lunch, and was played to the jury by video. Under Victorian law, this kind of recorded interview is known as a VARE —Visual and Audio Recorded Evidence statement. The VARE is taken by a specially trained police officer. It serves as a child's evidence-in-chief at trial, sparing them the trauma of giving evidence in open court. Although it is possible for the child to be cross-examined under controlled conditions, in this case, neither Ben nor Kate was.

Kate's interview, recorded on 16 August 2023, was shown first. She was sitting on a blue armchair. There was a small side table with a box of tissues and some colouring pencils nearby. The chair seemed so large against her small frame. Her feet barely touched the ground. In the video, a police officer explains how the interview would work. The then nine-year-old became emotional. She didn't understand why she was being interviewed. Then, after some gentle guidance she indicated her understanding that they were going to talk about "the lunch."

In a small voice she told the officer, "I wasn't there, so I don't know what happened." She went on to explain that her mother had told her the lunch was to discuss "adult stuff" with the guests.

In the dock, Erin watched the footage on the small screen fixed in front of her. Her daughter, close up, filling the frame. It was one of the rare occasions during the trial where Erin showed visible emotion. Her eyes welled with tears.

The interviewer asked Kate whether her parents were separated. Kate didn't understand the question, replying, "They're husband and wife." She agreed they didn't live together.

She confirmed that, on the morning of the lunch, her mother had told her that she and her brother were going to the movies. She also recalled seeing food in the oven that morning, but didn't know what it was.

She said her mum told her she was unwell the next day.

"How many times do you think she went to the toilet?"

"I saw her go like 10 times."

When asked about the plates at home, she paused. "There's a black-and-red one, and there's some white ones… and I think that's all the colours we have."

As the video played, Erin wiped her nose with a tissue.

Kate was asked where they went the day after the lunch. She replied that they didn't go anywhere. She couldn't remember.

When the video ended, Beale adjourned until the following morning, and the jury was led out. In the dock, Erin struggled to maintain her composure. She took a deep breath, looked up toward the ceiling, and spoke a few words of self-soothing.

When court resumed the following morning, Ben's interview was played. His interview was recorded in the same room as Kate's had been. He was sitting in the same blue chair. Ben was fourteen years old. The chair didn't seem quite as big as it did during Kate's interview.

The interviewer asked Ben about his parents' relationship. He replied that it was "very negative." He said his father did things to try to hurt his mother. Asked to explain, Ben said his dad didn't like that his mum had changed his school recently, and had wanted to be on the paperwork for the school.

He said, "Dad wouldn't talk to mum about that."

As she had when she watched Kate's testimony, Erin watched Ben's testimony with tears welling in her eyes.

Ben's interview then moved to the day of the lunch. He confirmed helping bring the plates and drinking glasses to the kitchen after the guests left, and stacking them by the sink. Asked what the plates looked like, he described them as "plain white" and about 15 cm in diameter.

He told the interviewer that later in the day he had played video games with his friend Baldwyn, while his mother built Lego.

He said he had come downstairs the morning after the lunch to find his mum drinking coffee at the dining table. She told him she was feeling sick and had been up during the night with diarrhoea. He thought she was a bit quieter than usual.

He confirmed they had leftovers — steak, mashed potatoes, and green beans — for dinner the following night. He commented on how nice the steak was. When asked how he knew they were from the meal the day before, he replied that his mother had told him they were.

He confirmed the car trip to Tyabb for the cancelled flying lesson. He had no recollection of a roadside toilet stop. He was unaware that his mother owned a dehydrator, but he did recall her taking a photo of mushrooms while walking in the Korumburra Botanic Gardens during the COVID lockdowns. "I remember mum took a picture of them because she thought they looked nice," he said, describing it as a "fond memory." He detailed how he and Erin had discussed how mushrooms grow with trees and support each other.

He confirmed that Simon had come and collected him and his sister from school and took them to hospital.

"In the end, it was nothing," he said. He didn't feel unwell, and had returned to school on Wednesday.

In the dock, Erin reached for a tissue. She looked up at the ceiling, fighting back tears as her son's voice filled the courtroom. Through Anna's grief, Matt's quiet composure, the clinical detail of organ failure — she had given nothing away. But the sight and sound of her own children had clearly affected her.

The court then heard a read-in statement from Ben's friend, Baldwyn, the boy who had gone to the movies and McDonald's with the children. He recalled seeing plates in the kitchen sink when they arrived back at Erin's home that afternoon. From what he could remember, the backs of the plates were white.

38 MEDICAL EVIDENCE

THERE WAS significant and detailed testimony from a variety of health professionals.

Doctor Chris Webster had been the doctor on call at Leongatha Hospital on the morning of 31 July 2023. He had been treating Ian and Heather Wilkinson since the previous day, and had received Dr Morgan's early morning call warning of grossly abnormal liver function and suspected death cap poisoning. When Erin arrived at 8:05 a.m. and rang the doorbell, he quickly recognised her as "the chef of the meal."

Webster told the court he had shared his concerns about death cap poisoning with her, and asked where the mushrooms came from. She said Woolworths. He testified that she didn't ask him any questions about what potential exposure to death cap mushrooms might mean for her. She didn't ask to see Ian or Heather, who were just metres away. He shared his alarm when other staff told him that, five minutes later, she was gone — discharged against medical advice.

He testified about his three calls to her mobile phone. About the voicemails he had left, including the last one, where his message said he would have no choice but to contact police. He told the court about his call to triple zero. The recording was played to the jury and entered into evidence.

Webster then detailed Erin's return. How he had pressed her to bring the children to hospital after she said they had eaten leftovers. He was concerned that they may have been exposed to the same toxin. Erin resisted. She didn't want them scared.

His evidence painted a picture of a woman who was detached — she asked no questions, showed no concern for her family members just metres away, and made decisions that defied medical logic.

The Crown relied heavily on Webster's evidence. A woman who believed she had accidentally poisoned people would not walk out of a hospital within five minutes of being told she had been exposed to a potentially fatal toxin. A woman genuinely frightened for her children would not resist having them assessed. And the fact that a doctor had been compelled to call police to retrieve a patient for life-saving treatment was, Rogers argued, extraordinary — a measure of just how abnormal her conduct had been.

The defence did not directly attack Webster's credibility. He was an experienced rural GP. Instead, they sought to soften the implications of his testimony. Erin's rapid departure could reflect panic, confusion, or her well-documented distrust of hospitals. The Woolworths answer might have been a reference to where she bought some of the ingredients, not necessarily all of them. And her hesitation about the children could reflect shock or denial rather than concealment.

After the verdict, Webster gave several media interviews in which he made inflammatory remarks about Erin. The medical regulator took a dim view. But those comments were never part of his sworn testimony, and the jury never heard them.

A succession of other Leongatha Hospital staff gave evidence about Erin's two presentations on the morning of 31 July.

Kylie Ashton, who took Erin's observations on arrival, testified that Erin repeatedly insisted she could not stay — she was adamant. Ashton testified that she asked Dr Foote for assistance to help convince Erin to stay at the hospital.

Dr Veronica Foote testified about her attempts to stop Erin from leaving, and about her examination of the beef Wellington leftovers that police had collected from Erin's outdoor bin after she gave permission over the phone. CCTV footage was shown to the court, and entered into evidence, showing Foote, gloved hands, removing the leftovers from a Woolworths bag, spreading them out on white paper, and photographing them. She testified that Erin's elevated heart rate and blood pressure were consistent with anxiety or stress.

Under cross-examination, Foote conceded that Erin's symptoms may also have been consistent with poisoning.

Nurse Cindy Munro, who had been caring for Ian and Heather, was direct. "She didn't look unwell like Heather and Ian," she told the court. "I recall Ian being so unwell that he could barely lift his head off the pillow, and

Heather was a little bit unsteady on her feet, but Erin was sitting up. On the bed. She didn't look unwell to me."

Paramedic Eleyne Spencer gave evidence about the ambulance trip when Erin was transferred from Leongatha to Monash — a trip of one hour and thirty-nine minutes. In response to prosecution questioning, Spencer described Erin as "chatty, calm and nonchalant", noting that she was able to get onto the stretcher unassisted. Spencer told the court that Erin described having had diarrhoea between twenty-five and thirty times over the previous two days. Spencer said she told Erin to let them know if she needed the toilet during the journey, and that Erin did not ask once.

Spencer said that Erin had told them she had a headache at a pain level of seven out of ten. The paramedics administered intranasal fentanyl — a powerful opioid painkiller. It was considered a safer option given paracetamol might affect the liver-protecting medication Erin had been given earlier.

In a subsequent text message to Simon, Erin subtly pointed to the administration of fentanyl as evidence of just how unwell she had been. But from Spencer's evidence, it appeared to have been administered solely on the basis of Erin's self-reported pain — not because doctors believed she was critically ill.

Registered nurse Lisa Shannon, the after-hours coordinator at Korumburra Hospital, told the court that, on arrival, Don was considerably sicker than Gail. His condition worsened throughout the morning — medications failed to stem the diarrhoea, and a blood test revealed a dangerously high lactate level, a marker Shannon told the court could indicate metabolic disorder, liver failure, or sepsis. Both he and Gail were transferred to Dandenong Hospital.

Doctor Beth Morgan, medical registrar at Dandenong Hospital, gave detailed evidence about the night she spent treating Don and Gail. She told the court Don had presented with thirty to forty episodes of vomiting and diarrhoea. He was sweaty and distressed, but alert. His vital signs were relatively stable. It was the bloodwork that alarmed her — early signs of tissue damage and what she believed was evidence of liver injury. Gail, assessed by a different registrar, had initially appeared less ill and was admitted to a short-stay unit. But follow-up tests told a different story — worsening metabolic acidosis and rising lactate levels.

Morgan testified that, during the night, she had called the toxicology registrar, Dr Mark Douglas, multiple times as Don's condition deteriorated and that he had guided her to secure silibinin. She shared details of her call to the pharmacy. By then, she was also in contact with Leongatha Hospital about Ian and Heather's deteriorating condition, so she had told the pharmacist they would probably need enough for at least four patients. The pharmacy didn't have it. They would have to obtain it from another hospital.

Dr Douglas told the jury he had devised the initial treatment plan for Don, including N-acetylcysteine — known as NAC — to protect his liver, and had instructed Morgan to monitor Gail closely. He consulted a senior toxicologist, Dr Yit Leang, who initially concluded there wasn't enough evidence to warrant administering silibinin, the specific antidote for death cap poisoning. But by 6:50 a.m., with Don's condition worsening further, Douglas told the court he had come to the view that *Amanita* poisoning was more likely than food poisoning. NAC offered general liver protection, but silibinin worked differently, blocking the toxin's uptake into liver cells. This was why he had told Morgan to source it.

Morgan and Douglas' evidence carried weight beyond the clinical detail. The prosecution used it to underscore a critical point: While doctors were fighting to identify the toxin through the night, Erin — who later admitted she had begun to suspect foraged mushrooms may have ended up in the meal — said nothing. She told no one. The information that could have accelerated the diagnosis and treatment sat with the one person who had reason to suspect what had gone wrong.

The defence turned the doctors' uncertainty back on the prosecution. If trained doctors had initially treated the patients for gastroenteritis, then Erin's failure to raise the possibility of mushroom poisoning did not necessarily point to guilt. It could just as easily reflect the confusion of someone who, like the doctors themselves, had not yet made the connection.

Dr Conor McDermott, the toxicology registrar who had spoken to Erin by phone from the Austin Hospital, confirmed his account of the conversation he'd had with her when he called her on behalf of Poisons Victoria — the Woolworths claim, and the unnamed Asian grocer in the vague suburb.

He added that he had also spoken to Leongatha Hospital staff. "I was told that she complained of diarrhoea, like the other patients, but I was told also that this had not been observed while the patient was in the department." The defence challenged his recollection. McDermott held firm.

The doctors who treated Erin during her time in Monash Medical gave similar testimony. Dr Laura Muldoon found no clinical or biochemical evidence of Erin having *Amanita* poisoning. Dr Varuna Ruggoo confirmed Erin's liver function tests were all within normal limits. Both described a woman who appeared clinically well.

Professor Andrew Bersten's evidence went to two questions the prosecution needed answered under oath. The first was cancer. He gave detailed testimony outlining his review of Erin's medical records. He confirmed there was no record of a cancer diagnosis, no appointment for an MRI, no needle biopsy. Erin's supposed medical crisis was now provably false.

Bersten was asked for his professional assessment of Erin's condition after lunch. He said her records showed mild symptoms consistent with a diarrhoeal illness — elevated haemoglobin and low potassium — but he had found no evidence of liver injury, and no evidence of acute illness on 30 July. Under defence questioning, he conceded her symptoms were consistent with dehydration. He reconfirmed possible diarrhoeal illness. Under prosecution re-examination, he affirmed those symptoms were consistent with genuine illness — but notably, not death cap mushroom poisoning.

Professor Stephen Warrillow, Director of Intensive Care at Austin Health, had the unenviable task of sharing with the court the extent of the victims' suffering, and the lengths to which hospital staff went to try to save them. The jury had heard, through earlier witnesses, how Don, Gail, Heather, and Ian had deteriorated. Now Warrillow described it in the language of intensive care — the intubations, the mechanical ventilation, the organ failure that resisted every intervention. Don's liver transplant had bought time, but nothing more. "He got relentlessly worse," Warrillow told the court. "We had no other treatments to offer."

He shared details of Heather and Gail's decline. Heather died from altered liver function and multiple organ failure, with a clinical diagnosis of *Amanita* mushroom poisoning. Gail died the same day from multiple organ failure resulting from altered liver function, also clinically diagnosed as *Amanita* mushroom poisoning. Don died from "refractory multiple organ failure secondary to altered liver function". In other words, his organ failure was resistant to treatment even after the liver transplant. The clinical terms were slightly different for each. The cause was the same — death by death cap mushroom.

In the public gallery, members of the Patterson and Wilkinson families wept quietly as the final moments of their loved ones' lives were described.

Of Ian, Warrillow told the court, "We thought he was going to die. He was very close." Ian was in the courtroom, listening to the testimony of his own near-death.

The defence had no questions for Warrillow.

Forensic pathologist Dr Brian Beer had performed the autopsies on all three victims. He gave evidence describing the pattern of injuries in each case — extensive necrosis of the liver — "very consistent" with *Amanita* poisoning. Don's autopsy showed evidence of a failed transplanted liver. Unlike Gail and Heather, traces of both alpha-amanitin and beta-amanitin were detected in Don's postmortem samples. Beer noted that Don had mild hypertensive heart disease, and was slightly overweight, but confirmed neither had contributed to his death. In the dock, Erin sniffled as Beer described the autopsy findings.

Taken together, the medical evidence established a devastating contrast. Four guests were in intensive care with catastrophic organ failure. Erin, perhaps mildly unwell, had spent a single precautionary night in hospital.

39 THREE TESTS. ONE POISON

IN THE THIRD week of the trial, the evidence moved to what the science could prove. The prosecution called a series of expert witnesses focused on what was in the beef Wellington leftovers that police had fished out of Erin's bin.

Dr Tom May was the prosecution's key mycology witness. Coincidentally, he also appeared elsewhere in the evidence. He was the author of one of the death cap articles found on Erin's computer, as well as the author of one of the iNaturalist posts that the prosecution contended that Erin had read and actioned.

Using May as an expert witness was unsurprising though. He is the Principal Research Scientist in Mycology at the Royal Botanic Gardens Victoria, author of the major catalogue volumes in the *Fungi of Australia* series, and is the country's foremost authority on mushroom identification.

May started his evidence by walking the jury through a slide show. He used this to simplify and explain the science behind how mushrooms grow and how death caps are identified. He took them on an educational journey — where death caps are most commonly found in Australia, and how they form what he called "an obligate relationship" with trees from the oak family. That is, they are only found close to oak, beech, and chestnut trees. He also told the jury about the narrow window of time they can be found in Australia — April and May.

He confirmed his own iNaturalist post about the Outtrim death cap sighting on 21 May 2023.

Rogers, for the prosecution, showed the court a series of photographs recovered from the Samsung tablet seized from Erin's home — mushrooms on dehydrator trays sitting on a set of kitchen scales. In one photo, the scales showed a weight of 210 grams. She pointed out the metadata on the photos to the jury. Last modified 4 May 2023.

She turned to May. Pointing to an oversized image on the large screen at the front of the court, she asked him if the mushrooms in the photo were death caps.

He replied that he believed they were consistent with death cap mushrooms, "at a high level of confidence." But he added a caveat, saying there were potentially other mushrooms that look similar when presented in this way.

Rogers sat, and defence junior Sophie Stafford stood to cross-examine May.

She showed him a series of ten different photographs of mushrooms and asked whether they were consistent with death caps.

May said that there were "many challenges" in trying to identify a mushroom from a single image.

Stafford jumped on his concession. "We simply don't

know whether those mushrooms are toxic until someone consumes them, isn't that right?"

"That is generally a way that we determine the mushroom is toxic. After ingestion and connecting symptoms," he replied, "but it is also possible to analyse mushrooms for known toxins, so that would be another way."

Stafford pressed her point, asking whether he agreed that poisonous mushroom identification was "fraught with challenges." He agreed. He also agreed that misidentification was the cause of the majority of accidental mushroom poisonings.

She showed him the mushroom photos he had discussed with the prosecution earlier in his testimony. She endeavoured to have him dilute his statement that they were potentially death caps.

"I can't say with any degree of certainty that they're not death cap mushrooms," he replied.

He repeated his earlier concession that identification from photos was challenging, but held firm on his "high degree of confidence" that those particular images were of death caps.

She had no further questions.

Stafford's cross-examination had been skilled, but it couldn't dislodge the high likelihood that the photos found on her client's device were of death cap mushrooms.

Rogers' re-examination for the prosecution was brief. May confirmed that fresh death cap mushrooms have no particular smell, but once dried, they develop a very strong and unpleasant odour.

May's testimony complete, he stepped down.

Christine McKenzie, the retired poisons specialist who

had found the death caps in Loch and posted them to iNaturalist gave evidence confirming her iNaturalist post. Shown one of her own photographs, she remarked, "If I may say so myself, that's quite a nice image of a death cap mushroom." The courtroom laughed. She told the jury that she had tried to reduce the risk by removing as many death caps as she could see.

Stafford stood for the defence. She asked McKenzie a series of questions regarding whether she had ever seen death caps growing at the Loch reserve before the day she photographed them. McKenzie replied that, based on the location and tree varieties in that area, she had long suspected it would be an ideal location for death caps to grow. She agreed that April 2023 was the first time she had actually observed them there. McKenzie confirmed she had removed every death cap she could find, but agreed she had not returned to the site afterwards. She could not say whether more had grown.

On broader identification, McKenzie was candid. She described herself as a 'novice' when it came to non-toxic mushrooms. From her years at the Poisons Information Centre, she knew the toxic ones quite well, but beyond that, she said, "I'm as much in the dark as anybody else."

With McKenzie's testimony done, the prosecution turned its attention to the beef Wellington leftovers. After being retrieved from the garbage bin outside Erin's home, they had passed through three sets of scientific hands. Each expert had used different methods of forensic examination. Each had come to a different conclusion.

Dr Camille Truong entered the witness box. Rogers led for the prosecution.

She displayed a number of evidence photographs on the courtroom screens. The images showed two blue plastic Ziploc specimen bags, with portions of leftover beef Wellington sitting nearby. Each bag bore labels that identified them as pertaining to the "Patterson" investigation. They were the lunch remnants from Erin's bin. One of the food scraps looked like a squashed sausage roll, the other like a partly eaten pasty.

Truong confirmed she worked as a mycology research scientist at the Royal Botanic Gardens. She was a colleague of May's.

She told the court that she had been the on-call mycologist for the Victorian Poisons Information Centre on 31 July 2023 — two days after the lunch — and that she was the first to forensically examine the leftovers. She told the court that the specimens had arrived at her office after she had left for the day, so she had them sent to her home. That evening, she cleaned a bench, set up a small microscope, and used tweezers to pick out tiny pieces of mushroom from the samples. She examined them again at her office the following day. She said that on both occasions she could identify field mushrooms — *Agaricus bisporus*, the kind sold in supermarkets — but found no death cap remnants.

Mandy stood. He asked Truong if she had told Dr Muldoon at the time that there had been "absolutely no sightings of death cap mushrooms in Victoria during the preceding couple of months."

She had.

David Lovelock, a diagnostics manager with Agriculture Victoria Research, was the next witness. He told the court he had examined the fruit platter, the gravy, and seven vials of debris scraped from the dehydrator trays. He had also analysed the beef Wellington leftovers, but he had used a different method than Truong. Using a DNA barcoding process, Lovelock found no death cap traces in the leftovers, the fruit platter, or the gravy. But two of the seven tiny debris samples from the dehydrator returned positive — a 99 per cent match to *Amanita phalloides*. He had found death cap mushroom DNA inside the machine Erin had dumped at the tip.

The defence did not challenge his findings.

Before the next witness was called, Justice Beale addressed the jury. He had received information that, in breach of his directions, one of them may have discussed the case with people outside the jury room. He stressed he had not made a positive finding that this conduct had occurred, but equally, he could not dismiss the possibility. He needed to protect the integrity of the trial. One juror was discharged. The jury was now fourteen.

Victoria's chief toxicologist, Dr Dimitri Gerostamoulos, from the Victorian Institute of Forensic Medicine, was called next.

Lenthall led for the prosecution.

Gerostamoulos told the court he had undertaken chemical analysis of the beef Wellington leftovers and the debris from the dehydrator. He wasn't looking for mushrooms. Rather, his analysis was looking for the poison itself. He confirmed his testing had found clear evidence of alpha- and beta-amanitin, the chemical signatures of death cap toxin. It was present in both the mushroom paste, as well as in meat, from the leftover beef Wellington. He had also found death cap toxins in four of the seven dehydrator debris samples. The toxin had survived the cooking. It had survived the chopping, and the blitzing. But it was there.

Lenthall asked Gerostamoulos to share with the court what the approximate dose of *Amanita* toxin would be required to kill a human. He replied that it was 0.1 milligrams per kilogram of body weight. For a person weighing 70 kilograms, that meant roughly half a death cap mushroom was likely to be fatal.

Gerostamoulos confirmed that Don and Ian had tested positive for death cap amatoxins. Gail and Heather had not, though no urine sample had been taken from Gail. Erin's results were also negative.

Lenthall had no further questions. She sat down.

Mandy rose for the defence. He took Gerostamoulos back to Erin's negative toxicology results, and the fact that the prosecution had relied on them as a strong indicator that she hadn't eaten the poisoned food. Mandy wanted to give the jury another way to read those same results.

He pressed Gerostamoulos on the timing. The guests had been tested between 25 and 32 hours after the lunch. Erin's pathology samples were taken 51 hours later — almost a full day behind. Gerostamoulos agreed that the sooner a sample was collected, the better the chance of detecting the toxin.

Mandy then turned to outcomes. He had Gerostamoulos agree that the amount consumed, the concentration of toxins in the meal, and individual factors such as age, health, weight, and what Gerostamoulos called 'toxic response' could all affect how a person responded to the same poison. Two people could eat the same contaminated meal. One might die. The other might survive.

Lenthall rose for re-examination. She started to put a theoretical poisoning scenario to Gerostamoulos.

Mandy objected immediately.

It was late in the day, so Beale decided to adjourn. He told the court they would come back to the objection the following day.

When the court reconvened the following morning, and Gerostamoulos returned to the witness box, Mandy withdrew his objection.

Lenthall put her scenario to Gerostamoulos: If two adults, with no serious pre-existing health conditions, consumed the same amount of the same meal containing death cap mushrooms, and one of them died, what would be the expected health outcome for the person who had survived?

Gerostamoulos replied that there was a high likelihood of an adverse outcome for the survivor. He noted that it was not necessarily hypothetical — it had happened the previous year in Victoria. Two people had consumed the same meal. One died, and one had survived. He restated that individual outcomes depended on how much was eaten and the individual's response to the toxins.

In the dock, at the rear of Courtroom Four, Erin, wearing black-rimmed glasses, studied the screen in front of her intently. Her face was devoid of emotion. Unreadable.

40 PINGS, PINS AND PASSWORDS

DOCTOR MATTHEW SORELL entered the witness box on 19 May. Sorell is principal of Digital Forensic Sciences Australia, an Adelaide-based specialist forensics consultancy. The court heard he had previously testified in over 400 criminal matters, and that one of his areas of expertise was mobile phone network data. He was a well-credentialled expert witness.

Warren, for the prosecution, led his examination.

Sorell began by giving the jury a lesson in telecommunications. He explained what cell towers are — the infrastructure that provides a radio connection between a mobile phone and the network. He told the jury that cell towers, also known as base stations, could be located on a variety of structures, including telecommunication towers, commercial buildings, grain silos, or even large water tanks.

"In an urban environment, these are spread out throughout the suburbs," he said. "In country areas, there are typically one to two cell towers that cover a local town, then there will be cell towers designed to cover the areas between towns. We end up with a relatively large number of cell towers, placed carefully throughout that environment," he said.

He explained that analysis of call charge records and event-based monitoring records can be used to trace the movement of a specific phone. Both data sets are held by the telecommunications provider independently of the mobile phone. In other words, it is possible to track a phone's movements without needing to have the physical handset or SIM.

He explained that call charge records provided basic details relating to calls, texts, and data usage. Depending on the frequency and duration of phone use, there might only be one call charge record created every fifteen minutes or so. Event-based monitoring records, related to signalling — the phone communicating with the network — were created with far greater frequency. In a metropolitan area, for instance, a phone might make five to ten of these records every minute.

It was dry, but important, background to help the jury understand the significance of the conclusions he was able to draw from the data that he had analysed.

Warren then asked a series of questions where Sorell confirmed he had been provided with four-and-a-half years of call charge records, from January 2019 to August 2023, relating to a phone belonging to Erin. He had also been provided a much narrower, but highly targeted, series of event-based monitoring records, including 28 April and 22 May 2023. Two dates of particular interest to investigators.

With context now established, Warren took Sorell to Erin's phone records for 28 April 2023. This was ten days after Christine McKenzie had posted her death cap sighting at Loch to iNaturalist.

The jury was shown a large map of the Gippsland area. Cell towers, depicted by circles, were marked on the map. Sorell was careful to point out that the size of the circles was not an indicator of the area of coverage.

Sorell said the call charge records indicated a possible visit by the mobile phone to Loch, originating from and returning to Korumburra, no earlier than 9:06 a.m. and no later than 10:07 a.m. that day.

"When you look at the event-based records, it gives us more refined detail," he said. The records beamed up on the big screen. Sorell pointed out the relevant pattern of connections. The phone had connected to cell towers at Loch or Loch South at 9:08 a.m., 9:09 a.m., and 10:01 a.m. In other words, the phone lingered in or near Loch for about an hour.

Warren then moved to 22 May 2023 — the day after Dr Tom May had posted his Outtrim death cap sighting to iNaturalist.

Sorell testified that, on this particular morning, phone records from Erin's phone showed it had first connected to the Loch South cell tower "about every five minutes" from 9:19 a.m. until about 10 a.m. "While it could be moving in and around that area, it could not have been moving very far," he said. The connections were consistent with the phone remaining "relatively stationary" in or near Loch. Warren needed the jury to understand the significance of what they were hearing. She looked directly at them, and reminded them that Christine McKenzie had found, photographed and removed death caps in Loch just one month prior.

Sorell continued. He said that by late morning, the phone moved from pinging cell towers near Loch and had started pinging towers near Outtrim. This was consistent with a car journey from Loch to Outtrim. He told the court his initial analysis, undertaken on call charge records, led him to conclude that the phone had simply moved through Outtrim, possibly on the Bass Highway.

But he changed his mind when he analysed the event-based monitoring records for that date.

Warren brought up a map on the courtroom screen to help Sorell explain the details.

Between 11:18 a.m. and 11:49 a.m. Erin's phone had connected to the Outtrim cell tower eight times. It briefly touched nearby towers between those connections, but it kept returning to the Outtrim cell tower. Sorell told the court he couldn't say exactly where the phone had been, but he was confident it had remained in the Outtrim area until 11:49 a.m., before the connection moved back to cell towers in Leongatha at around midday.

The Outtrim cell tower was located in the northern-most part of the map. Sorell pointed out Neilson Street for the jury — the location where Dr May had observed the death caps. It was nearby, to the south of the Outtrim cell tower.

"Possibly, there was a visit to Neilson St at that time," he observed.

Warren then took Sorell to the phone records from 31 July — two days after the lunch, the morning Erin had presented to Leongatha Hospital and left after five minutes.

Sorell said the records from that morning were "most consistent" with the mobile phone being to the west of Leongatha, although it had connected with an Outtrim cell tower for about three minutes at 8:55 a.m. The Outtrim tower was in the opposite direction from Erin's home.

He said a visit to the Outtrim area was "not strongly supported" though, because the records were silent as to the location of the phone after 8:58 a.m. "There is a gap in the records of about 30 minutes," he said. The phone may have been switched off. It may have been out of range. Sorell couldn't say.

Warren then asked Sorell about the broader pattern of phone movement. Over the fifteen months from January 2022 to April 2023, how many times had Erin's phone shown connections consistent with possible visits to Loch?

Sorell confirmed eight possible visits.

And to Outtrim?

Five possible visits.

The large screen at the front of the court flickered, then stopped working. Beale asked the jurors to continue to follow the evidence on their court-issued iPads instead.

Under cross-examination by Colin Mandy SC, Sorell was first asked about the behaviour of mobile phones in the area. Mandy asked whether it was common, in the years of call charge records he had analysed, to see the mobile phone switch between two cell towers in quick succession.

Sorell agreed it was common. In those instances, he

said, the phone may not have moved — one cell tower may have just "temporarily dominated over the other."

Mandy asked whether, during his analysis, Sorell had observed instances where the mobile phone appeared to be stationary in Leongatha but was connecting with cell towers in Outtrim or Mirboo North.

Sorell accepted that there were times this had happened — movement within Leongatha, with a fleeting connection to the Outtrim cell tower. "Generally speaking, when those more distant connections occur in a hurry, the phone may not be moving very far away from the Leongatha area, but those more distant connections denote some movement, although not large movement," Sorell said.

Mandy turned to the 28 April records. He put it to Sorell that there were no records showing the mobile phone was definitely within the boundary of the Loch township.

Sorell agreed — but added a qualification. The records showed the mobile phone was certainly to the east of the Loch township.

Mandy then turned to the 22 May records. He asked whether the records from that day were consistent with the proposition that the mobile phone "moves from Leongatha, down the Bass Highway, heading to Inverloch, and at some point remains stationary for a period of time."

Sorell pushed back. The township of Kongwak sits on the Bass Highway midway between Leongatha and Inverloch. If the phone had been travelling from Leongatha to Inverloch, he would have expected it to connect with the Kongwak cell tower along the way. It didn't.

"That's an anomaly that doesn't fit with your proposition," he said.

However, he did concede the possibility that the mobile phone did not enter the Outtrim postcode area on 22 May. "There are locations outside the Outtrim postcode where this set of records could conceivably come up," Sorell said.

The court was shown a topographical map of the Outtrim area. The Outtrim cell tower was more elevated than the nearby Koonwarra and Leongatha cell towers — a detail that could affect which tower a phone connected to.

Sorell looked down in front of him. "Nice little beetle crawling across the microphone," he observed.

It was a moment of levity in what was dry and technical testimony.

Sorell's evidence had been careful, qualified, and honest. He had not overstated his findings. He had spoken of possible visits, not confirmed ones. He had accepted that routine travel could explain some tower connections, that topography and weather could affect results, and that a phone could sometimes connect to a tower up to sixty kilometres away.

But the data had also resisted Mandy's attempts to explain it away entirely. The Kongwak anomaly sat uncomfortably against the innocent drive-through theory. The eight event-based monitoring connections across thirty minutes on 22 May were difficult to reconcile with a car that was simply passing through. And the coincidence of the dates — phone near Loch ten days after an iNaturalist death cap post, phone near Outtrim the day after another iNaturalist death cap post. A dehydrator purchase that same afternoon. A series of strong coincidences that no amount of cross-examination could erase.

Warren called her next witness for the prosecution: Senior digital forensics officer Shamen Fox-Henry, from the Victoria Police cybercrime squad.

Fox-Henry started his testimony by confirming he had started working for Victoria Police in October 2020, and had joined the cybercrime squad in July 2023 — the same month as the fatal lunch.

Like Dr May, Fox-Henry had also prepared a slideshow for the jury.

Its first slide read, "What is a computer?"

Fox-Henry was not prepared to risk making assumptions about what the jury members may or may not know about computers. He started with the absolute basics and worked up from there. He explained CPUs, storage devices, write blockers, and digital copies. He walked the jury through the process to remove the internal storage of a computer, connect a write blocker to avoid damaging the data, create a digital copy, process the copy to interpret the data, and then export the results in a non-editable format.

He then defined the terminology that would recur throughout his evidence. Artefacts — a file, a folder, or an internet search. Cookies — small files generated by web servers to tell websites about the user. Favicons — the small icons associated with websites. Thumbnails — small images representing larger ones. He finished by explaining what metadata is, and the difference between "created," "modified," and "accessed" dates and times.

It was painstaking. Necessary. And entirely unglamorous. But by the time Fox-Henry had finished his tutorial, the jury had the understanding and vocabulary they would need to follow his evidence.

On behalf of the prosecution, Warren moved into a series of background questions. She asked Fox-Henry about how the Magnet Axiom application worked.

She asked him to expand on his analysis of the Cooler Master computer seized from Erin's home. He said the first thing he did was "extraction processing." There were three storage devices, or hard drives, inside the computer. He created copies of each, then, using the Magnet Axiom application, ran a series of keyword searches over the data — death cap, death cap mushroom, death cap mushrooms, mushrooms, and poison.

Warren then displayed a subset of the report with his findings. One page of the report showed four "search query" records relating to the search term "iNaturalist" on 28 May 2022, at about 7:20 p.m.

Fox-Henry walked Warren through the sequence. At 7:20 p.m. on 28 May 2022, a Bing search was made on the Cooler Master for 'iNaturalist'. By 7:21 p.m., the browser had navigated to inaturalist.org. At 7:23 p.m., the user clicked through to a specific page — a death cap mushroom sighting at Bricker Reserve in Moorabbin that had been posted ten days earlier. Fox-Henry confirmed that that particular page had a visit count of two. It meant that the person viewing the page had visited it twice. Then there was a second browser search. Also at 7:23 p.m.: 'Korumburra middle pub'.

Fox-Henry had also examined a Samsung tablet belonging to Erin. The jury was shown photographs extracted from it — a photo of a black dehydrator, and two photos of mushrooms on the trays of the dehydrator. The metadata showed "last modified" dates of 30 April 2023 and 4 May 2023 respectively. Four screenshots from an internet browser were also extracted from the tablet, with three referring to ovarian cancer.

Fox-Henry confirmed he had examined a second Samsung mobile phone, which had been seized from a wardrobe in an upstairs bedroom during the August raid. The phone had still been logged into a Facebook account under the username 'ErinErinErin.' It hadn't been wiped or factory reset. It yielded all of Erin's Facebook Messenger chat threads. Among them were the messages Erin had shared with her small online friend group in late 2022 — the hostile, profane outbursts about Simon and his parents written during the child support dispute.

"I said to him about fifty times yesterday that I didn't want them to adjudicate," she had written, followed by an eye roll emoji. "Nobody bloody listens to me. At least I know they're a lost cause."

And, "Don said they tried to talk to him but he refused to talk about it so they're staying out of it but want us to pray together. I'm sick of this shit I want nothing to do with them."

There were others too — the "fuck 'em" message, the swipe at Gail for being horrified about the child support claim. Now twelve strangers were reading them all on a courtroom screen.

Fox-Henry confirmed he had examined Phone B — the Samsung Galaxy A23 that Erin had handed to police on 5 August. He told the court that his analysis showed that four factory resets had been conducted on the device — on 12 February, 2 August, 5 August, and 6 August 2023. He testified that the August resets had resulted in the phone being "irreversibly wiped."

Then it was over to the defence.

Mandy started by establishing Fox-Henry's experience. Fox-Henry conceded that when he received Erin's devices for examination in August 2023, his training in the specialist software he had used was limited to instruction received from another officer.

Mandy took Fox-Henry to the question of whether files found on Erin's devices could have arrived there without her knowledge. He agreed that applications like Telegram could be set to automatically download — that content posted in a chat or channel could find its way onto a device without the user interacting with it.

"They are cached within the program itself," he said.

Signal worked the same way, Fox-Henry agreed. WhatsApp too. Facebook Messenger — "Yes, very similar."

It was a significant concession. If files could arrive on a device automatically, then the mere presence of poison-related material on Erin's computers and tablets did not necessarily mean she had sought it out. At least, not for every file.

Mandy then turned to the AppCache strings — the cached fragments that Fox-Henry had recovered from the Scorptec computer. Among them was a string containing the words "Deathcap (*Amanita phalloides*) iNaturalist," associated with the Google Chrome browser.

When asked in cross-examination what the string indicated, Fox-Henry was candid. "That that string was present on that device on the date of the creation of that file," he said.

Mandy pressed further. Did the string provide any information about user interaction with that entry?

"Not that I'm aware of, and nothing that I'd be confident answering," Fox-Henry replied.

On the Monday morning of Fox-Henry's fourth day in the witness box, the trial's most bizarre interruption occurred. A man in the public gallery jumped to his feet. He was wearing a yellow T-shirt with the slogan *all we are saying is give truth a chance* in black letters. He addressed Beale directly. "How can you be a judge?" he demanded, before making a reference to "concealed crimes." He got no further. Security moved quickly. The man was escorted from the courtroom before most of the gallery had registered what was happening. The jury watched in silence. Beale said nothing. Proceedings resumed as though the interruption had never occurred.

Mandy turned straight back to Fox-Henry and continued his line of questioning, asking what the user would have seen on the computer when the string was created.

"It would be purely speculation. All I can determine from this string is that that path is present on the computer, and it appears to be associated with Google Chrome."

Mandy turned to the two PDF documents recovered from the Samsung tablet — the appendix on common homicidal poisons and the article on red kidney bean poisoning. He asked whether the records could demonstrate that these files had been automatically downloaded to the device.

Fox-Henry initially said, “I don’t know for certain.” But when pressed, he examined the file directory path and gave his considered answer. “Based on that directory alone, it looks like that item has been downloaded to the phone.”

“Automatically, or not?” Mandy asked.

“Based on that directory alone, not automatically.”

“How are you able to say that?”

“The path directory doesn’t reference a cache that I would expect to see associated with Facebook Messenger.”

It was a subtle but important distinction. The AppCache strings — fragmented, ambiguous, potentially automatic — were one thing. The poison PDFs were another thing entirely. They sat in the download directory. Someone had deliberately downloaded them. Fox-Henry wasn’t going to say otherwise.

No further questions. Fox-Henry stepped down.

41 CLOSING THE GAPS

NOT EVERY PROSECUTION witness delivers a bombshell. Some are called to authenticate exhibits, confirm the chain of custody, make sense of timings, or close small gaps the defence might otherwise exploit.

Rogers understood the necessity of this work. Proving a case beyond a reasonable doubt requires more than compelling witnesses and dramatic evidence. It requires proof that every exhibit was handled properly, every timeline is accurate, and every loose end has been tied up.

As part of their evidence, the prosecution entered a CCTV timestamp accuracy table. This was necessary to explain time discrepancies across the CCTV footage entered into evidence. The Leongatha Hospital timestamp was one hour and 42 minutes ahead, which explained why the footage appeared to show Erin leaving the hospital at 9:52 a.m., when the testimony of multiple witnesses had placed her departure at 8:10 a.m. Subway Leongatha's cameras ran one hour behind. The BP Caldermeade and

Koonwarra Transfer Station videos were time-stamped correctly.

Sally Ann Atkinson from the health department and Troy Schonknecht, an environmental health officer from Monash City Council, gave evidence about what Rogers called the 'wild goose chase' — their efforts to track down the Asian grocery store Erin claimed to have bought dried mushrooms from. Atkinson told the court she had spent days trying to get Erin to narrow down the location — calling, texting, being ignored. She told the jury how each time she spoke to Erin, the suburb kept shifting. Schonknecht shared that he had physically visited fourteen stores across three suburbs over two days, finding nothing that matched Erin's description.

Under cross-examination, Schonknecht conceded that he had never checked stores in Glen Waverley. He said he wasn't asked to. This conflicted with Atkinson's testimony that she had asked him to check Glen Waverley. Mandy would later highlight to the jury in closing that, "One of them is honestly mistaken."

Atkinson also told the court how, unable to reach Erin by phone on the Wednesday after the lunch, she had requested Cripps call her when she visited Erin's home for a prearranged meeting.

Cripps gave evidence next. She told the court about her initial conversation with Erin at Monash Hospital, where Erin had described Don and Gail as "the parents she never had". Cripps also recalled a specific detail from Erin's account of Saturday evening. Erin had told her she had been so unwell when she dropped Ben's friend home that she had been, in her own words, "sitting down, acting like a cork to prevent an accident." Erin had characterised Simon as controlling. Erin told Cripps the purpose of the lunch had been to see the family and reconnect. She said Erin never mentioned cancer to her.

Cripps went on to tell the court that on 2 August 2023, at Atkinson's request, she had called Atkinson once she reached Erin's home and handed the phone to Erin so Atkinson could speak to her. Cripps said that, during this visit, again at Atkinson's request, she had asked Erin if she could look through her bank statements for any transaction that might identify the Asian grocer where Erin claimed to have purchased the dried mushrooms. Erin had replied that she had checked her bank records and couldn't find any purchase relating to mushrooms, saying she was likely to have paid cash for such a small item.

Darren Canty, Operations Manager at the Koonwarra Transfer Station, told the court how police had contacted him on 4 August and asked him to check the e-waste bin. He sent an employee to retrieve the only item matching the description police had given — a black Sunbeam dehydrator. Ben Goodwin, a forensic officer, gave evidence via video link. He confirmed he had examined the dehydrator after its recovery from the tip, using tweezers to extract seven samples of possible vegetable matter from the trays, placing each into a specimen jar, and sending them to AgriBio for analysis.

Senior fingerprint specialist Sonia Geremia told the court she had lifted latent fingerprint impressions from the rear of the dehydrator and compared them to prints taken from Erin. They matched her left index, middle, and ring fingers.

It was Tuesday 27 May 2025 when Rogers called the prosecution's last two witnesses.

Detective Sergeant Luke Farrell of the Homicide Squad took the stand. He confirmed he was the officer who had coordinated the search of Erin's home on 5 August 2023. He shared details of the raid with the jury — the dehydrator manual in the kitchen drawer, the Cooler Master computer in the upstairs bedroom, the cookbook with its food-spattered beef Wellington page.

He testified that at the conclusion of the search warrant, he had asked Erin to hand over her mobile phone. She had offered him two possible passcodes — one four digits, one six — and said she couldn't remember which was correct. When Farrell went to enter the first, he found the phone was already unlocked. No passcode had been set.

The police video of this exchange between them was played to the jury. In it, Erin sat at the dining table in a beige jumper, her face propped in one hand, elbow on the table. She put on her glasses and leaned across to watch Farrell handle the phone.

Farrell told the court that a further search warrant was executed at Erin's house in Mount Waverley later that afternoon. It was a property she had purchased in 2019 with part of her inheritance from her mother. Erin had been in the process of preparing it for sale. No one was present. No items of interest were found. The search concluded at 5:40 p.m.

Under cross-examination by Mandy, Farrell acknowledged that police had not photographed all of the plates found in Erin's home, and had not seized any of them. He also agreed that when he told Erin during the search that two people had died, she did appear surprised and had asked who had died.

Mandy had no further questions. Farrell stepped down.

The man who had owned the case from the beginning was next. Fittingly, he was the Crown's final witness.

Detective Leading Senior Constable Stephen Eppingstall of the Homicide Squad — the appointed Informant — had sat behind the prosecution team every day of the trial. As Informant, he was permitted to remain in court during other witnesses' testimony, an exemption routinely granted to the lead investigator so they can monitor how the evidence unfolds. Now, after weeks of watching, it was his turn in the witness box. He chose to stand.

Warren led his examination. Over two days, she walked Eppingstall through the framework of the investigation the jury had been hearing about for weeks — but from the perspective of the man who had directed it.

He confirmed the four sets of CCTV footage police had gathered: the BP at Caldermeade, the Subway in Leongatha, Leongatha Hospital, and the Koonwarra Transfer Station. He took the jury through the Woolworths Everyday Rewards data — the three shopping trips in six days, each time purchasing the same core ingredients for the same meal.

He said Erin's medical records contained no evidence of a cancer diagnosis, no appointment for a needle biopsy, and no referral for an MRI. The text messages between Erin and Gail — in which Erin had claimed to have undergone these very procedures — were displayed on the courtroom screens beside the medical records that contradicted them.

He walked the jury through the phone evidence. He confirmed that Phone A — Erin's primary device, the one she had used to communicate with everyone in her life — had never been recovered. Carrier records showed its SIM card had been removed on 5 August, while police were searching Erin's home. The SIM moved into a Nokia handset that was never recovered either. He said that Phone B, the device Erin had handed to police, had been used for data in a Samsung tablet up until 3 August 2023. It had never been used for a phone call until the day of the raid.

He confirmed that the seized Cooler Master computer had been the device on which the iNaturalist searches were made — the Bing search, the navigation to the death cap sighting at Bricker Reserve in Moorabbin, and the Korumburra pub order two minutes later. The jury was shown a screenshot that Eppingstall had taken of the iNaturalist page in December 2024, though Beale reminded the jury that the page may have changed between May 2022 and when the screenshot was taken.

Eppingstall told the jury that Dr Tom May had alerted police to his own Outtrim death cap sighting during the investigation — a detail that explained how investigators had come to focus on that location.

Warren entered into evidence, then played the video recording of Eppingstall's August 2023 interview with Erin at Wonthaggi Police Station. The jury watched Erin deny foraging and deny owning a dehydrator — lies her own barrister had already conceded in his opening address. They also heard her give a phone number that wasn't hers. In the dock, Erin watched herself on the small screen.

Little of what Eppingstall had shared in his evidence-in-chief was new. The jury had heard it all before — from the forensic analysts, the mycologists, the digital examiners, the doctors. But none of them had seen the full picture. Eppingstall had. His evidence took the scattered threads of their testimony and wove them into something that felt more like a cohesive narrative.

Mandy's cross-examination of Eppingstall ran across three days. His strategy was not to challenge the evidence itself — it was to challenge the completeness of the investigation. He picked at what hadn't been done, what hadn't been seized, and what hadn't been obtained.

He established that, with the exception of the single vehicle accident when she was younger, Erin had no criminal history.

He had Eppingstall concede that Erin had been somewhat cooperative in the early stages of the investigation — directing police to the leftovers, providing her gate code, and retaining the fruit platter and gravy. He then moved to the search warrant. Eppingstall confirmed he had remained with Erin for the majority of the search, but that she had been given approximately twenty minutes alone in a room with the door closed to contact her lawyer. Eppingstall admitted he couldn't say what had happened behind that closed door.

Mandy brought a police photograph up on the large screen. It was one that had been taken during the search.

It was an image of devices and charging cords sitting on an ottoman. He suggested one of the items was Phone A.

Eppingstall disagreed.

If it had been a phone, he said, it would have been seized.

Not to be deterred, Mandy brought up another photo. This time, he pointed out a black item on the kitchen windowsill, suggesting that it might be Phone A. Eppingstall said he didn't think the object was consistent with a phone.

"It's a matter for the jury," Eppingstall said.

Mandy brought up another photo. He suggested two laptops in this image had also been missed, along with a USB stick that had been stored in the pantry.

Eppingstall was direct. "If they're laptops, this is the first I'm learning of these items," he said of the first. And of the USB, "I wasn't searching, sir. I was with Erin."

On the bank records, Mandy landed a concession. Police had only obtained Erin's records from 1 July to 4 August 2023.

"No other periods of time?" Mandy asked.

"No," Eppingstall replied. Then, candidly, "And I can't explain why we didn't go back further."

Mandy challenged the scope of the cell tower analysis. The jury had heard Dr Sorell had been given multiple years of call charge records, but only about twenty days of the more granular event-based monitoring data. Mandy asked why more wasn't obtained. Eppingstall was honest. "To get EBMs for a year, we would be talking well into six figures, and my boss isn't real keen when I spend too much money." The courtroom laughed. "We have to be selective and targeted," he added.

Mandy took Eppingstall back to the Facebook Messenger messages. To the "fuck 'em" and "lost cause" exchanges that the jury had already heard read aloud during Fox-Henry's evidence. But this time, Mandy wanted to give some context.

He pointed to the messages surrounding Erin's outbursts — her online friends sharing their own problems, offering sympathy and sharing frustrations. Eppingstall agreed the chat was one where participants were "venting to each other about various issues in their lives." It was a small concession, but it served Mandy's purpose: These weren't calculated statements of murderous intent. They were the words of a frustrated woman seeking solace in an online support group.

Then Mandy played his strongest card. He took Eppingstall to Erin's medical records from 2021 — records that the prosecution had tendered. In one, a doctor had written, "Erin worries about ovary cancer, has been googling her symptoms, thinks her symptoms may be suggestive of ovary cancer." Another record noted a family history of ovarian cancer — both a paternal aunt and a maternal aunt. Neither note proved that Erin had cancer, but they did lend support to her claim of having cancer-related anxiety. It had been documented by her doctor a number of years before the lunch.

On redirect, Warren asked Eppingstall about the target for searches when a warrant is executed. He replied that police aim to seize all electronic devices — tablets, phones, USB sticks. Anything with storage.

Warren sat down. Eppingstall was excused. After four days of evidence, he had been methodical, candid about the investigations limitations, and careful not to overstate what the evidence could prove.

Rogers stood. For the benefit of the jury, she read the agreed facts — including that Erin's fingerprints were on the dehydrator. She sat down. The prosecution rested.

By now, the trial had been running for five weeks. Morwell had settled into the strange rhythm of a small town hosting a national event. With only two cafes within walking distance of the courthouse, the lunch break geography was unavoidable. Defence barristers, prosecutors, witnesses, and reporters all ended up in the same places, standing at the same counters, sometimes shoulder to shoulder. One journalist later recalled waiting for a coffee next to Ian Wilkinson — the man who had survived the lunch and had been a quiet, steady presence throughout the trial. She wondered whether she should say something. Then she remembered — three people had died, and he was still grieving. She let him be.

42 THE SOLE WITNESS

IT WAS 3:12 P.M. Justice Beale looked toward the defence table. "What course will the accused be taking?"

Colin Mandy rose. "Your Honour, the defence will call Erin Patterson."

A hush fell over the courtroom. The jury was swiftly ushered out.

For eighteen minutes, Court Four waited.

When the jurors returned, something had changed. The dock at the back of the room — where Erin had sat for twenty-four days, flanked by prison officers, watching proceedings on a small screen — was empty. She was now seated in the witness box, facing the jury directly for the first time.

She took an affirmation rather than a religious oath, and sipped water from a paper cup as she settled in.

In a murder trial, the defence's job is to dismantle the Crown's case. To create a reasonable doubt. They do this by challenging evidence, exposing weakness, and calling their own expert witnesses to analyse and offer a counterinterpretation of key evidence. They often do this without calling their client — the accused — to give testimony at trial.

Many people charged with murder retain their right to silence — right up to and including the trial. This prevents their own words from being used against them. It stops the prosecution from questioning them in front of the jury. The prosecution cannot call the accused as a witness against themself. Their only chance to directly question the accused comes if the defence calls them to testify in their own defence. And that is a strategy that is not without risk. Veteran Melbourne criminal barrister and former Chief Magistrate Nicholas Papas KC, who was not involved in the case but was approached by Reuters for independent comment, was quoted as saying that calling the accused to testify is a rare strategy, and is normally done only as a last resort. "You're actually putting the case in the hands of your client, and lawyers don't tend to want to necessarily do that. We like to control the process if we can," he said.

Through his cross-examination of the prosecution's witnesses, Mandy had already done some solid work — a question here, a concession there — chipping away at the Crown's case to highlight doubt for the jury. He didn't need much. Just enough doubt.

Erin's hair was down. She was wearing a dark paisley top and dark pants. She had worn this same shirt a number of times before.

She looked at the jury. Waited for the questions to begin.

Mandy started gently. He began by asking Erin what her life had been like in July 2023.

She replied that her children had just started at a new school, had made new friends quickly, and were coping better than expected.

He then moved into a series of questions about her and Simon's relationship, her conversion to Christianity shortly after she met Simon, and the care arrangements for the children. How they could see Simon whenever they wanted. He asked her to describe her relationship with Simon in late 2022. "Functional," she replied.

He asked about her relationship with the Pattersons. She said she had felt distance growing between her and her in-laws. She blamed Simon. She had concerns that he didn't want her involved in his family "too much." She said she felt she was "being left out of things."

She talked of her ongoing battle with low self-esteem, and said that at the time of the lunch she was contemplating gastric bypass surgery.

She spoke of the birth of her first child in Perth. It had been, she said, a very traumatic experience. The labour went on for a very long time. When the baby wouldn't come, they had to do an emergency caesarean. She cried as she described it. And then, weeks later, Don and Gail had come to visit. Gail had been supportive and kind. Erin became emotional again at the memory of it.

She talked of the trip from Perth to Townsville, where she had left Simon and flown back to Perth alone. She said it was "a lot harder" travelling with the baby. "I'd had a gutful."

Of her and Simon's separation, she said, "I didn't want

to be separated, but I felt there was no choice." She shared that, although it was hard in the immediate aftermath, they had gone back to being really good friends.

He asked what her relationship was like with Don and Gail after the separation. With her voice breaking, she said, "It never changed. I was just their daughter-in-law, and they just continued to love me."

Of the children's relationship with their grandparents, she said, "They were very close. Especially Ben and Don. They were like two minds separated by 50 years. Ben just loved him." Her voice was trembling as she fought back tears again.

It was a portrait Mandy was carefully constructing — a woman bound to this family by mutual love and shared history. No estrangement. No resentment.

With the background established, Mandy moved to more personal issues. Her weight. Her relationship with food. She became visibly emotional. Tissue in hand, her chin quivered. Erin said that she had never had a good relationship with food. Her mother had weighed her weekly as a child. "I've tried every diet under the sun." She shared that she was bulimic. That since her twenties she would eat "everything she could get her hands on" then make herself sick. She said this was her secret. Not even Simon had known.

Mandy asked who else knew. She paused. "Nobody. Nobody. Everybody now, but nobody knew then."

He asked if she had ever been diagnosed with ovarian cancer.

"I have not."

Had she ever had a needle biopsy on a lump on her elbow.

"I've never had a needle biopsy anywhere."

She had a reason for lying to Don and Gail about the MRI and the needle biopsy. Through tears, "I did lie to them." But it was because her in-laws had shown her a lot of care, which had "felt really nice." "I didn't want their care for me to stop."

She could explain the faked cancer diagnosis too. She was planning weight loss surgery and was embarrassed to tell them. She had anticipated needing time in hospital and wanted their help with the children, but couldn't bring herself to share the real reason. "I was ashamed of the fact that I didn't have control over my body or what I ate," she lamented.

Mandy took her to the series of messages between Erin and her Facebook friends. He displayed the "This family, I swear to fucking god" message. Erin said the Facebook group was a safe venting space. "I wish I'd never said it," she told the court. "I feel ashamed for saying it, and I wish the family didn't have to hear that I said that. They didn't deserve it."

He brought up her "I'm sick of this shit" and "fuck 'em" messages. Erin sighed. Sniffled. She replied that, in the messages, she was being dramatic. She had played up the emotion to get sympathy from her online friends.

He took Erin back to other messages previously shown to the court — the Signal text message argument between her and Simon around his mother's birthday. The text series that included Erin refusing to come, Simon berating her, and the apology for yelling at him. She dismissed this as no big deal. Just how they did things. "I would feel hurt. We'd be annoyed at each other for a day or two, then we'd calm down and apologise," she said.

Mandy showed her the photos she had sent to her Facebook friends of mushrooms laid on a dehydrator shelf. She remarked about one photo, "Looks like they're at the end of the cycle." She confirmed that she had developed an interest in wild mushrooms during COVID in early 2020. Her interest had been sparked by seeing mushrooms during walks with her children in the Korumburra Botanic Gardens. He asked her what she enjoyed about mushrooms.

"They taste good, and they're very healthy."

"Why wild mushrooms?"

"They just taste more interesting. More flavour."

She said she would purchase them at Woolworths and at markets, and sometimes buy dried mushrooms from Asian grocers. She would use a mixture of wild and store-bought dried mushrooms in curries, pasta dishes, and soups.

She detailed her early, tentative foraging efforts. She said it took her a number of months to build up the confidence to cut up, fry, and eat mushrooms that she had foraged herself. She said she would also hide mushrooms in her children's meals, cut up small so they wouldn't notice.

Mandy went back to her foraging. She said she had foraged for mushrooms in May of 2023 and had dehydrated them. He asked where she had stored them. Erin replied that she had placed them in a plastic container along with some store-bought dried mushrooms.

He moved to the beef Wellington, asking Erin directly, "Do you accept there must have been death cap mushrooms in there?"

"Yes, I do."

He asked where the mushrooms in the beef Wellington came from.

"The vast majority came from the local Woolworths in Leongatha, and there were some from a grocer in Melbourne," she replied.

Mandy noted that the jury had previously heard evidence that she reported buying dried mushrooms from an Asian grocer. Erin agreed, but said she couldn't remember the exact purchase, though she was certain it was during the April school holidays.

She described adding some mushrooms from her plastic container to the beef Wellington as she prepared the duxelles, the mushroom paste. She had wanted to improve its bland flavour.

She accepted there was a "possibility" she had unintentionally added foraged mushrooms to the beef Wellington.

The story unfolding in Erin's evidence was vastly different to what she had told police during her interview in 2023.

Shown photos from the SD card that police had seized, she explained the images of toxic mushrooms by saying she had become aware of poisonous mushrooms growing in her local area and had wanted to ensure her dog didn't eat them. Mandy took her to further images from the card showing wild mushrooms. She had photographed these to figure out what variety they were. Erin became emotional and patted her eyes with a tissue when photos of her children appeared among the series of photos shown to the court.

Mandy moved to the evening of the lunch. Erin told the jury that diarrhoea had begun late that night — between 10 p.m. and midnight, every twenty minutes or so. By Monday morning, she claimed, she was unable to "retain" fluids and had decided to go to hospital.

She revisited her earlier bulimia disclosure, revealing that as she cleaned up after her guests had left, she couldn't help herself. She progressively ate all that remained of the orange cake that Gail had brought to the lunch — two-thirds of a cake. Then, feeling over-full and ashamed, she had forced herself to bring it all up in the toilet.

Mandy took her to the Sunday. The day after the lunch. When she had driven Ben to the cancelled flying lesson. Yes. She remembered. She explained to the court that she was still sick. The diarrhoea hadn't subsided. She said she had taken Imodium before the drive, but it hadn't worked. During the car trip she was forced to pull over and use the toilet in the bush. She cleaned herself up with tissues, placed them in a dog poop bag, and put it in her handbag. She stopped at a service station, where the CCTV had shown her brief visit to the bathroom. She said she went into the toilet and disposed of the soiled tissues, then bought food for her children. Nothing for herself. She also confirmed the stop at the donut van on the way home. She said she had asked Ben to buy her a drink — and he bought her a coffee. She said she didn't ask for coffee, so she assumed that Ben had bought it out of habit. She confirmed that, as soon as they got home, she had rushed inside to the toilet.

Mandy asked her about the following morning — presenting at Leongatha Hospital and leaving after five minutes. Erin said she had been caught off guard. She hadn't expected to be told she needed an overnight admission to a Melbourne hospital. She had animals at home that needed feeding. Her daughter had a ballet bag that needed packing. She wasn't prepared. She went home, had a brief lie-down, and then drove herself back to the hospital. She had never intended not to return.

Mandy's questions moved to her time in hospital. She described a conversation she claimed took place with Simon at Monash Medical Centre on 1 August. The children had been with them, but had left the room at some point, leaving her and Simon alone. According to Erin, Simon had accused her of using the dehydrator to poison his parents. Voice quivering, she quoted him as saying, "Is that how you poisoned my parents, using that dehydrator?"

She told the court she had replied, "Of course not," but that his words had prompted her to reflect on the lunch — to wonder whether mushrooms she had foraged and dehydrated might have mistakenly found their way into the meal.

Simon, in his own earlier testimony, had denied the conversation ever took place.

She also had an explanation for her apparent efforts to avoid the calls and messages from the health department in the days after the lunch. Erin said that Atkinson's repeated questions about the ingredients in the lunch made her feel "very anxious." She added that, by Tuesday after the lunch, and after Simon's accusations, she herself had begun to think that "perhaps the foraged mushrooms were in there too."

Mandy showed Erin a photo, taken by police during the search, of her kitchen. In the image, there was a black item on the windowsill. Mandy asked what the black item was. Erin didn't hesitate. She replied that it was a black phone case. With her usual handset — the Samsung Galaxy A70 — in it. She didn't explain the fact that, according to evidence previously shown in court, her usual phone had actually been in a pink case.

Erin told the jury that when she returned home after her August police interview, she found Phone A sitting on the kitchen windowsill. She said she was puzzled that police had not taken it. According to her evidence, she removed the SIM card from Phone A and placed it into the Nokia handset.

Quizzed about where her A70 handset was now, Erin replied that she threw it out as it had a cracked screen. She said she may have thrown it in the skip bin she had arranged in September 2023 for "an annual spring clean." She didn't explain why she had not simply had the phone repaired. It was, after all, quite new.

Mandy then took Erin to the four factory resets of Phone B. She had an explanation for each.

She said at the start of the year Ben had damaged his own phone, so he had used Phone B temporarily. He had reset it sometime in February to remove her data so he could use it.

The first factory reset that Erin admitted to doing herself was on 2 August at 11:09 a.m. She said she wiped it to remove Ben's data from the phone — he had taken it on a school camp and dropped it in mud. She cleaned it, charged it, and factory reset it. What she did not mention — but the prosecution later did — was that this reset was performed just minutes before she drove to the Koonwarra Transfer Station to dispose of the dehydrator.

Her second factory reset was on 5 August at 1:20 p.m. — during the police search of her home. Erin admitted it was her. She said she panicked. "I knew that there were photos in there of mushrooms and the dehydrator and I just panicked and didn't want them to see them." She maintained that the photos were quite innocent but would make her look bad.

Mandy asked if Erin had performed any further next factory resets of Phone B. She replied that there was one other, at 5:16 a.m. on 6 August — the morning after the police raid. Erin said she had logged into her Samsung Find account and could see where all her devices were. "I could see my phone, and Ben and Kate's, and it was really stupid, but I thought, 'I wonder if the police have been silly enough to leave it connected to the internet', so I hit factory reset to see what happened. And it did."

It was a curious explanation for an action taken before most of the population had risen for the day.

Mandy then revisited Erin's police interview. He noted that an officer had asked her if she had ever dehydrated "food or anything," and she had replied, "No."

"Was that a lie?" Mandy asked.

"It was."

He then asked whether she had also lied about owning

a dehydrator or knowing anything about one in her house. Erin agreed that both denials were lies.

Mandy asked why.

"Well, I had disposed of it a few days earlier, in the context of thinking that maybe mushrooms I'd foraged or the meal I'd prepared was responsible for making people sick. Then on Saturday, police told me that Gail and Heather had passed away, and it was this stupid knee-jerk reaction to dig deeper and keep lying. I was just scared, but I shouldn't have done it."

Mandy asked if she had also lied to police about never foraging for mushrooms. Yes. She had lied. For the same reason.

He asked whether she had ever deliberately foraged death cap mushrooms.

"No."

Had she deliberately included death caps in the individual beef Wellingtons? No.

Did she lie about serving the leftovers to the kids? No.

Did she intend to kill, seriously injure, or harm her lunch guests? Shaking her head, her voice trembled as she replied. "No. I didn't."

Mandy was done. Over three days, he had walked his client through a myriad of self-admitted lies, and she had explained every one of them to the jury. She wasn't proud, but she had an answer for each. He gathered his papers.

"No further questions."

Erin reached for a tissue. Her time in the witness box had been, by any measure, a performance of controlled vulnerability. Tears. Remorse. An explanation — however improbable — for every mistruth. Mandy had given his client every opportunity to be human in front of the jury.

Nanette Rogers SC had watched it all. Now it was her turn.

43 CROSS-EXAMINATION

CROSS-EXAMINATION BEGAN on Thursday 5 June 2025. It was day 27 of the trial. It would be Erin's fourth day in the witness box.

Before proceedings commenced, Justice Beale covered some housekeeping. He told the jury the trial would likely run into eight weeks — it had originally been estimated at five to six. The jury absorbed this news without visible reaction. They had been at it long enough to know that nothing about this case was going to be simple.

Rogers rose.

She didn't muck around. She immediately accused Erin of lying in her police interview.

"It was a lie when you told police on that occasion that you didn't own a dehydrator. Correct?"

"Correct."

She had Erin confirm the photo of the vehicle at the Koonwarra tip was hers. Rogers brought up the next photo on the big screen, and asked if the dehydrator in the skip bin was also hers.

"I presume so."

Rogers looked confused. "And why do you presume so?"

"Unless somebody else put in a dehydrator as well as me, then I presume that's the one I put in."

Rogers told Erin that a number of samples taken from the dehydrator had tested positive for death cap toxins. "You knew they were death cap mushrooms that you'd been dehydrating, correct?"

"No, I didn't know that," Erin replied.

Rogers said Erin had lied to police because she knew she had used the dehydrator to dry death caps. "You were very keen to dispose of any evidence which might connect you with the possession of death cap mushrooms, correct?"

Erin disagreed.

She pressed further. "You lied because you knew if you'd told the police the truth, it would implicate you in the deliberate poisoning of your four lunch guests, correct?"

"No. No. That's not true."

Rogers then referenced Erin's evidence-in-chief. Erin had told her barrister that Simon's accusation about the dehydrator had gotten her thinking that she may have accidentally poisoned her guests with mushrooms she had foraged and dried. Yet she had remained silent. She hadn't shared this with anyone.

"Surely if you had loved them, you would have immediately notified the medical authorities?" Rogers asked.

"Well, I didn't," Erin replied.

Rogers observed that no, she hadn't. Instead, she said,

Erin had rushed out of Monash Medical Centre on the day she was released on 1 August, so she could get home and get rid of the evidence.

Erin disagreed again, explaining that she had panicked because of what Simon had said to her about poisoning his parents. Rogers reminded Erin of Simon's evidence to the court. He denied making this accusation. She accused Erin of fabricating the entire conversation. Of using it as an excuse to cover up the fact that she had been caught destroying evidence.

Rogers then turned to an earlier episode — the morning of 31 July, when Erin had first presented at Leongatha Hospital. She had stayed five minutes, signed a discharge form against medical advice, and left. Rogers wanted to know what she did next.

Erin said she went home to feed the animals and pack her daughter's ballet bag.

Rogers put to her Simon's earlier evidence that Erin had told him she lay down on the floor at home and fell asleep for 45 minutes. Erin confirmed she had a "lie down for a while."

"Surely, that's the last thing you would do in these circumstances," Rogers said.

"It might be the last thing you'd do," Erin replied, "but it was something I did."

Rogers pressed. Erin had been told by hospital staff that they suspected death cap mushroom poisoning. She agreed they had. And after hearing that, she had gone home and taken a nap.

"They didn't tell me it was life-threatening," Erin replied.

Rogers then put to Erin that it was not the fact that she'd had time to prepare for her hospital admission that had prompted her return. It was Webster's final voicemail. He had left a message telling Erin that he had no choice but to contact police and ask them to find her and bring her back. Rogers suggested Erin had returned only because she knew police were coming.

Erin disagreed.

Rogers then put the phone data to her — expert evidence from Dr Matthew Sorell placing Erin's phone on the Bass Highway, heading south out of Leongatha towards Outtrim, between 8:55 a.m. and 9:45 a.m. Rogers suggested Erin hadn't simply gone home — she had driven towards Outtrim.

Erin retorted, "The Bass Highway doesn't lead to Outtrim."

It was a curious thing for Erin to say, given that the fastest route from Leongatha to Outtrim follows the Bass Highway before cutting across via Leongatha South-Outtrim Road.

Rogers kept going. She suggested that Erin had spent the one hour and forty minutes that she was away from the hospital working out how to manage the situation she now found herself in. She hadn't expected doctors to detect death cap poisoning so quickly. She had assumed it would be treated as food poisoning.

Erin denied it. "You're saying I spent an hour and a half thinking? I'm sure I did some thinking in that time, but it was not about covering my tracks."

Rogers brought up exhibits that had previously been shown to the court. Photos recovered from a Samsung tablet seized from Erin's home. Yellow-tinged mushrooms on dehydrator trays, sitting on kitchen scales. Mycologist Dr Tom May had told the court the mushrooms were consistent with death caps at a "high level of confidence."

"I suggest to you that these were death caps that you foraged on or after 28 April 2023. Correct?"

Erin denied they were death cap mushrooms.

Rogers then pressed Erin over the reason she had given for the lunch.

"You thought Simon would be more likely to accept an invitation if he knew that his parents and Ian and Heather would be attending. Agree or disagree?"

"I would disagree with that."

Rogers took her to the gastric bypass surgery she had raised in her evidence-in-chief. She pointedly noted that this was the first time Erin had ever mentioned it — right here, in the witness box.

Erin replied that it was true. She even had a pre-surgery appointment booked at the Enrich Clinic in South Yarra for September 2023. It was the first time she had shared details of this appointment. There was a quiet rustling at the bar tables. Both legal teams noted the new information. The court moved on.

Rogers took Erin to forensic evidence showing that a computer seized from her home had been used to search the iNaturalist website in May 2022, navigating to a specific death cap sighting in Moorabbin. Erin conceded it was possible she had made the search, but said she didn't remember.

"I suggest you had an interest in death cap mushrooms

on the 28th of May 2022, agree or disagree?" Rogers asked.

"It depends on what you mean by an interest," Erin replied.

"Well, it's a very straightforward question, Erin," Rogers shot back.

Erin never got to answer. Beale interjected to stop the trial for the day. It was the end of proceedings on Friday, with the coming Monday being a public holiday. Rogers' question hung in the air unanswered.

When they returned to court the following Tuesday, Rogers went straight back to the gastric surgery and the appointment at Enrich Clinic. Over the weekend, the prosecution had obtained a statement from the clinic's office manager. Rogers put it to Erin directly. The Enrich Clinic was a cosmetic dermatology practice. It did not offer gastric bypass surgery. It did not offer gastric sleeve surgery. It had never conducted pre-surgery assessments for such procedures.

Erin replied that she was "puzzled." Her memory was that the appointment was for weight-loss surgery. Perhaps it was a different procedure. She had also been looking into having liposuction.

"When you gave sworn evidence to this jury last Friday that you had a pre-surgery appointment for gastric bypass surgery booked in for early September with the Enrich Clinic in Melbourne, that was a lie. Agree or disagree?"

"It wasn't a lie. That's what my memory was."

Rogers said Erin's medical records showed no referral

from her GP. There was also no MRI. No biopsy. No surgery planned.

Erin attempted to explain herself. Rogers cut her off. "I'm the person who asks the questions. If there's something that needs to be clarified in re-examination, your barrister will do so."

Rogers then displayed an iNaturalist post on the large court screen. She put it to Erin that on Monday 28 April, she had driven to Loch to find death caps after reading Christine McKenzie's iNaturalist post about a sighting there ten days earlier. She pointed to the expert phone evidence, which had placed Erin's phone near Loch that morning — in the same approximate area where McKenzie had photographed and geo-tagged the death caps.

Erin replied, "I don't know if I did go to Loch that day."

She also corrected Rogers on the date. "I don't mean to be argumentative, but I think the 28th of April was a Friday. I remember that because my daughter had a ballet concert that weekend."

Rogers said that Erin weighed the death caps on her kitchen scales to determine five fatal doses — one for each of the four lunch guests, plus one for Simon.

Rogers then displayed the receipt for Erin's dehydrator purchase, bought that same afternoon from Hartley Wells in Leongatha.

"Within hours of finding them," Rogers said, "you drove to Hartley Wells and bought a dehydrator."

"I did buy it that day, yes," Erin replied.

"And the purpose was to dehydrate death cap mushrooms."

"Disagree."

Rogers then put it to Erin that she had read Dr Tom May's post about death caps in Outtrim on 21 May, and driven there the very next day. "I suggest you went to Neilson St in Outtrim looking for the death cap mushrooms as posted by Dr Tom May."

Erin disagreed. She told the court she didn't believe she had travelled to Outtrim as a destination. She may have passed through it on the way to Inverloch or Wonthaggi.

Rogers challenged Erin's foraging narrative as a fabrication. A story she had invented for the jury to explain how death caps might have entered the meal once her Asian grocer story had collapsed.

Rogers pointed to the total absence of corroboration. Erin's own children had told police they had no recollection of their mother ever picking wild mushrooms. Thousands of text messages between Erin and Simon — but not one mention of foraging. More than 400 books catalogued in her home — not a single one about foraging or how to identify wild mushrooms.

Erin pushed back, saying she had "a lot more books than that" and that many were still packed in tubs in her garage at the time of the police search. She conceded though, that "probably" none were about foraging.

Rogers continued. No computer seized from her house had records relating to edible or non-toxic mushrooms. And not a single mention to any online friend before the lunch.

"That might be right," Erin replied. "I don't know if I told them or not."

Rogers said that Erin had lied to staff at Monash when she had denied going mushrooming. Erin took exception to the word "mushrooming." She said it could mean a couple of things — foraging, but also other uses of mushrooms not related to eating.

Rogers asked what she would call picking mushrooms for food.

Erin replied, "Pick and eat."

She would never use the word "mushrooming," Erin said. She would say "foraging."

Rogers put it to Erin that, even after learning her guests were gravely ill in hospital, she had never told a single doctor, nurse, or health official that foraged mushrooms might have been in the meal. Instead, after being discharged, she drove home and got rid of the dehydrator.

The cancer claim was next. Rogers pointed to screenshots cached on Erin's Samsung tablet showing internet searches about ovarian cancer and brain cancer, with metadata dates of May 2023. Erin had maintained throughout her evidence-in-chief that she had never told her guests she had been "diagnosed" — only that she might need treatment.

"This information from the internet, I suggest, would allow you to tell a more convincing lie about having cancer," Rogers said.

"I mean, theoretically, that's true. But it's not what I did," Erin replied. She said she had been genuinely concerned she had ovarian cancer and was also worried that there may be something wrong with her brain.

Rogers took Erin to Gail Patterson's diary, which had an entry on 28 June 2023 reading "Erin — St Vincent's — arm lump." Erin confirmed she had told Gail about a lump on her elbow. But she conceded she did not have a lump, did not have a cancer diagnosis, and had not had any appointments at St Vincent's.

"I didn't have a legitimate medical reason. That's true."

Rogers then displayed a text exchange between Erin and Gail from early July 2023. She read Gail's message asking how Erin's medical appointment went, then Erin's reply saying there was "a bit to digest" and promising to talk about it in person. Rogers pointed to its promise to share more face-to-face. It was sent nine days before Erin had invited Gail and Heather to the lunch. She accused Erin of sending the text to lay the groundwork. To ensure her guests attended the deadly lunch. Erin denied it.

She said she didn't have a specific reason to invite her guests. She just did.

Rogers then referred to Child Protection worker Cripps, who had told the court that Erin had told her the purpose of the lunch was, in part, to discuss a medical issues. "Cripps is wrong, is she?" Rogers asked.

"Yes," Erin replied.

Rogers took Erin to Ian's evidence, where he said that Erin had shared a cancer diagnosis at the lunch and was anxious about telling her children.

"So he was wrong too, was he?" Rogers asked.

Erin replied that he was confused.

Rogers said, "I suggest that you never thought you would have to account for this lie about having cancer, because you thought that the lunch guests would all die."

"That's not true."

Rogers took Erin back to her 2023 police interview. Erin had told police that Don and Gail were "the only family I've got."

Rogers launched a series of rapid-fire accusations — that Erin didn't truly love them, that she was angry they had sided with Simon in the child support dispute, and that she had publicly projected warmth toward them while privately expressing contempt.

"You had two faces," Rogers said. "A public face of appearing to have a good relationship with Don and Gail, and a private face — the one you showed in your Facebook Messenger chats, where you insulted them and mocked their faith."

"Incorrect," Erin replied.

Rogers said, "I suggest that you didn't love them."

"That's not true."

"I suggest you were angry they had taken Simon's side."

Erin shot back, "That's not true. I had a good relationship with Don and Gail."

Rogers suggested that Erin didn't regard Simon as a decent human being. Erin pushed back immediately. "Actually, I still believe that," she said. Her voice strained during the exchange.

Rogers then displayed the December 2022 Facebook group messages — "I'm sick of this shit I want nothing to do with them… so fuck 'em" and "this family, I swear to fucking god." She showed messages where Erin had responded to Don and Gail's advice to pray with emojis. Rogers said the emojis were eye-rolls and that Erin was mocking her in-laws. Erin disputed that they were eye-roll emojis, saying they showed a face with a straight line for a mouth.

"That is not an eye roll emoji. There are better ones for that. I wasn't mocking. I was frustrated."

They moved to the child support issues. Rogers displayed through the messages that had gone back and forth between the former couple in late 2022 via the family chat group on Signal. She wanted to know why Erin had insisted on copying Simon's parents into the dispute. Erin said she didn't want them to intervene. She just thought Simon's behaviour might change if he knew his parents were aware of it.

Rogers pointed to a message Erin had sent to Don, saying she wanted Simon to "do the right thing" by his children. Wasn't that asking them to intervene?

Erin faltered. "I think it was more of a global proposition. Whether he paid school fees or not, it wasn't going to change whether the children went to school or not. I'm finding it hard to explain what I meant by that."

And then the Asian grocer. Rogers walked through the shifting story Erin had told almost a dozen witnesses across 31 July to 3 August 2023. The dried mushrooms came from Woolworths, then also from a Chinese grocer in Oakleigh, then possibly Glen Waverley, then Clayton, then Mount Waverley — the suburbs changing with almost every conversation. Fourteen stores searched. Nothing that remotely matched Erin's description.

Rogers noted with interest that Erin had been able to share quite specific details about the packaging —

including the size and the label, yet she apparently had no memory of the shop. Or even the suburb.

To this point in cross-examination, Erin had, on a number of occasions, corrected Rogers on small details with notable precision. Rogers now used that same precision against Erin.

"You couldn't remember the location of the Asian grocer, yet your memory in this witness box has been remarkable. You could even recall that April 28 was a Friday, not a Monday. But you couldn't recall a shop you visited just a couple of months earlier."

Erin remained silent.

"This is a story you have made up for this jury. Agree or disagree?"

"Disagree."

She asked why Erin had described herself as not "very familiar with Glen Waverley" despite having a house nearby.

"I may have been being pedantic. I do that," Erin replied.

Rogers pointed to the Facebook messages — Erin telling her online friends she was blitzing mushrooms into powder and hiding them in food. She suggested Erin had been "testing how to hide mushrooms." Erin denied it.

Then came the sixth beef Wellington. Rogers put to Erin that she had prepared it for Simon — in case he changed his mind and attended — and that it too was poisoned.

"I didn't make the sixth one for Simon," Erin replied.

Justice Beale intervened, asking Erin, "Who did you make it for?"

"Just an extra one. Simon wasn't coming."

Rogers suggested that sometime after the lunch, Erin had removed the steak from inside the pastry then had put the mushrooms and pastry in the bin. Erin agreed, saying the steak was "put somewhere else."

Rogers asked where.

Erin replied, "In my children's stomachs."

Rogers put Ian's evidence to Erin — that the guests ate from four large grey plates while she served herself from a smaller, "orangey-tan" plate. She reminded Erin that Heather had independently raised the same concern with Simon on the way to hospital — puzzling over why Erin had served herself on a different plate.

Rogers said the different plate was a deliberate and calculated precaution — to ensure Erin didn't accidentally consume a poisoned parcel herself.

Erin was blunt. Ian had given "incorrect evidence." She didn't own grey plates or a matching set — she had simply taken the last plate left.

Rogers accused Erin of faking her illness after the lunch. She noted that not one medical professional had observed Erin appearing unwell in the way her guests were. Intensive care specialist Professor Bersten had found no evidence of *Amanita* poisoning or any other toxic substance in Erin's test results. Rogers said that all he found was slightly elevated fibrinogen. Consistent with stress, not poisoning.

"Disagree."

Rogers took Erin back to her claim that she had taken Imodium before the drive to Tyabb. Rogers said there was no record of this in her medical file, and that none of the staff recalled Erin mentioning it.

Erin agreed she hadn't told them, saying nobody had asked.

Rogers pressed. If she had genuinely gone to hospital seeking something stronger than what she had taken at home, she would have told them what she had already taken, along with the fact that it wasn't working.

Rogers then put the cake purging story to the test. She accused Erin of making this up as an excuse to cover the fact that she wasn't ill at a time that her guests were deathly ill. She asked Erin whether her evidence was that she had vomited up beef Wellington.

"I couldn't be sure what was in the vomit."

Rogers reminded the jury that the court had received no expert evidence that vomiting would prevent absorption of the toxins. Nor anything that might have established how quickly it would need to occur.

Rogers noted that Erin had never mentioned making herself vomit after eating cake to any of the medical professionals who had seen her after the lunch, despite being specifically asked about her symptoms.

She also said that Erin had told the court she struggled with binge eating and bulimia — yet there was no record of her disclosing this to her general practitioner. Ever.

She said, "You were not suffering from death cap mushroom poisoning. Correct or incorrect?"

"I have no idea."

"You knew how suspicious it would look if you did not seem sick like your guests. Correct or incorrect?"

"Incorrect."

Rogers reminded Erin of Dr Webster's evidence — she quoted him telling Erin that her children could be "scared and alive, or dead," and urging her to get them to hospital immediately. Rogers told the court it took Erin over an hour to arrange for Simon to collect them from school and take them to hospital. She put to Erin that her reluctance wasn't about protecting her children from stress — it was because she knew they hadn't eaten the poisoned food, and so were in no danger.

Erin disagreed.

Rogers reminded Erin of Ben's evidence about the day after the lunch. He had said that she had driven over an hour to Tyabb on 30 July without stopping once for the toilet, despite claiming she had diarrhoea.

Ben was mistaken.

Rogers continued. When Erin did stop at the BP service station in Caldermeade during this same journey, CCTV showed she spent just nine seconds in the bathroom before browsing the sandwich fridge. Rogers suggested that if she had truly relieved herself in the bush on the way, as she claimed, nine seconds was not enough time to even wash her hands.

Erin said nothing.

Rogers then turned to the leftovers. She put it to Erin that she had lied — over multiple days, to multiple people — about feeding her children the leftover beef Wellington with the mushrooms scraped off.

Rogers noted that by the evening of 30 July, Erin already knew Don and Gail were in hospital and had told her own son she "thought it might have been the lunch." Why, then, would she feed those same leftovers to her children? Rogers suggested she hadn't — because she knew the food was poisoned and would never have risked her children's lives.

Erin disagreed.

Rogers put it to Erin that Phone A — her primary device throughout the critical months — had been deliberately concealed from police because it contained data that would implicate her: iNaturalist searches, death cap research, evidence of foraging activity. She noted that Phone A's SIM card lost connection with the network sometime between 12:01 p.m. and 1:45 p.m. on 5 August, while police were searching Erin's house. Rogers accused Erin of removing the SIM card during the time she was alone, supposedly calling a lawyer.

Erin disagreed, saying the call to her lawyer happened at 2 p.m. She said she moved the SIM card much later, after she had returned home from her police interview and found Phone A on the windowsill, untouched by police.

"Nonsense," Rogers snorted. "I suggest it's because you deliberately concealed this phone from police."

"Disagree."

Rogers then went to the various factory resets.

"I suggest that you did three factory resets of this phone, Phone B, to conceal the true contents, so you could then pass off Phone B as your usual mobile phone, without police realising."

Erin agreed she carried out the resets, but she denied she did so for the reasons Rogers suggested.

Rogers then walked Erin through the testimony of witness after witness called by the Crown — people whose accounts Erin had contradicted over her five days under cross-examination. Ian Wilkinson on the plates. Her own son on whether she had been drinking coffee the morning after the fatal lunch. Dr Webster and Nurse Ashton on conversations at the hospital. Each time, Erin's position was the same. They were wrong, confused or mistaken. Rogers didn't need to spell it out. The pattern spoke for itself — by the end of her evidence, Erin had disputed the recollections of nearly a dozen people.

Shortly after 11:30 a.m. on Thursday 12 June, Rogers told the jury she had three final questions. She delivered them in rapid succession.

Had Erin deliberately sourced death cap mushrooms in 2023?

"Disagree."

Had she deliberately included them in the beef Wellington meal she had served her guests?

"Disagree."

Had she done so intending to kill them?

"Disagree."

Rogers sat down.

Throughout her cross-examination, Erin had corrected Rogers on syntax, on days of the week, on various inconsequential details. She had challenged the premise of questions before answering them. She had asked Rogers to repeat herself when questions weren't to her liking. But for all her combativeness, many of her answers were single words — "agree," "disagree," "correct," "incorrect" — delivered over and over in flat monotone. It suited Rogers though. Every word Erin had uttered gave her a little more content that she could stitch into her closing argument.

Mandy rose for re-examination.

He was brief. He took Erin back to the Enrich Clinic, producing a screenshot from its website showing it had previously offered liposuction. He then displayed a text message confirming Erin had booked an appointment. The message showed Erin's appointment was intended to be with a clinician named Priscilla Auyeung, but was cancelled on 11 September 2023.

"Do you accept now that you were mistaken about the Enrich Clinic offering gastric bypass surgery?" Mandy asked.

"Yes, I was obviously mistaken," Erin replied.

Then he asked her about her children. About the flying lesson that had been cancelled the day after the lunch. Her voice broke. She began to cry.

When Mandy finished, Erin delivered her own closing words from the stand, "I did not intend to poison anyone. I did not intend to harm anyone. I did not intend to mislead anyone."

Then, without waiting to be dismissed, she stepped down from the witness box and walked back toward the dock. Head down. Tears in her eyes. Tissue in hand.

"Just wait there, Ms Patterson," Justice Beale said.

She kept walking.

He called again. This time she stopped. Turned. Walked back to where she had been.

But it was over. Eight days in the witness box. Five of them under Rogers. The relentless "agree or disagree," the pointed "correct or incorrect."

All of it, done.

The defence case, with its sole witness, now rested.

44 CLOSING ARGUMENTS

CLOSING arguments are each side's final opportunity to address the jury directly. No new evidence can be introduced. The prosecution closes first, setting out its case and urging the jury toward conviction. The defence follows — deliberately given the last word — with the intention of raising enough doubt to prevent conviction.

In a case like Erin's, built almost entirely on circumstantial evidence, the closing addresses carried particular weight. There was no confession. No eyewitness to the preparation of the poison. Everything turned on whether the jury believed the evidence, taken together, excluded any reasonable possibility of innocence.

Rogers went first. Over two days, she closed for the prosecution. Her delivery was structured and methodical.

She presented Erin as a woman with two faces. The Signal messages of warmth set against the Facebook messages of contempt. Publicly, the perfect daughter-in-law, mother, and wife. Privately, a petty, stewing woman who brooded over imagined slights.

Rogers drew the jury's attention to the fact that Erin had deviated from the recipe she claimed to have followed. The *RecipeTin Eats* cookbook called for a single beef tenderloin log wrapped in pastry. Erin made individual portions instead — six separate parcels, each fully encased. Rogers argued this was deliberate. Individual portions gave Erin control over what went into each serve, and ensured she would not accidentally eat a poisoned one.

"That choice to make individual portions — rather than the single log the recipe called for — allowed her complete control over the ingredients in each individual parcel," Rogers told the jury. "It is a control, the prosecution says, that she exercised with devastating effect."

She then introduced a framework of what she called the four calculated deceptions.

The first was the cancer fabrication — the lie that had assembled Erin's victims at the table. Rogers pointed to the ovarian cancer searches on Erin's tablet, arguing that she had researched the disease in advance of the lunch so she could tell a more convincing lie. She traced the deception from its earliest seed — the entry in Gail's diary in June that read "Erin — St Vincent's — arm lump" — through to the text message Erin had sent Gail nine days before the lunch, telling her there was "a bit to digest," and promising to share more in person. Rogers said the message was sent to lay the groundwork. To ensure the guests would attend. Rogers reiterated her belief that Erin had never thought she would have to account for the cancer story because she expected the lie would die with her victims.

Rogers said the second calculated deception was the

deliberate sourcing and preparation of death cap mushrooms. The iNaturalist searches. The trips to Loch and Outtrim. The purchase of the dehydrator on the same day that her phone placed her near the first site. Rogers told the jury that Erin knew exactly what she was looking for and had targeted her search accordingly. She reminded them of the total absence of corroboration for the foraging story — no books, no internet searches about edible mushrooms, no mention to any friend, and Erin's own children unaware that she had ever picked wild mushrooms, despite the fact that they lived with her.

The third deception was the simulated illness. Rogers said Erin needed to appear sick so suspicion would not fall on her. Rogers illustrated her point by drawing a series of devastating parallels — placing what was happening to Erin alongside what was happening to her guests at the same moment in time.

On the morning after the lunch, Ian Wilkinson was grey, stooped, and visibly unwell. Erin's son found his mother drinking coffee at the dining table. On Sunday 30 July, while her guests' conditions worsened, Erin drove her children a two-hour round trip to Tyabb.

By 2:30 p.m. on Monday 31 July, Don Patterson was critically ill and in multiple organ failure, on life support ventilation with a tube down his windpipe. Ian was so unwell that he could barely lift his head off the pillow, and Heather was unsteady on her feet, but Erin was sitting up on a hospital bed texting on her phone.

By 1 August, all four lunch guests were in the Austin Hospital ICU, on life support, their organs shutting down. Erin was discharged from Monash Medical Centre that same day. No clinical or biochemical evidence of *Amanita* mushroom poisoning. No liver damage. No toxic substance detected.

Rogers reminded the jury that not one medical professional had observed Erin appearing unwell in the way her guests were. Intensive care specialist Professor Bersten had found nothing in Erin's test results beyond slightly elevated fibrinogen — consistent with stress, not poisoning.

Rogers also dealt with the vomiting claim. Erin had told the court she purged after eating cake on the afternoon of the lunch — a product, she said, of her long struggle with bulimia and binge eating. Rogers noted that Erin had never disclosed bulimia to her GP. She had never mentioned vomiting to any medical professional who saw her after the lunch, despite being specifically asked about her symptoms. And the court had received no expert evidence that vomiting would have prevented absorption of death cap toxins, or how quickly it would need to occur.

Rogers then asked the jury a direct question. If you were told the meal you had cooked and served for your family possibly had death cap mushrooms, what would you do?

You would not go into self-preservation mode. You would not be reluctant to receive medical treatment. You would not take two and a half hours to agree to have your children assessed. You would tell treating doctors every skerrick of information you had.

But Erin hadn't done any of that. She had walked out of Leongatha Hospital five minutes after arriving, against medical advice, without receiving any of the lifesaving treatment doctors told her was time-critical. Rogers said the only reason she could have felt comfortable doing that was because she knew she had not consumed any death cap mushrooms.

Rogers argued Erin had never expected doctors to identify death cap poisoning so quickly. She had assumed the illnesses of her guests would be treated as food poisoning. When hospital staff told her, within minutes of her arrival, that they suspected death caps, Erin realised what she had done was going to be uncovered. She fled to buy herself some time. To work out how to manage the situation — and how to explain why she wasn't sick like her guests.

Rogers moved to the fourth calculated deception. The sustained cover-up. The lie about the children eating leftovers. The vague stories about the Asian grocer — a story that had shifted with almost every telling. Rogers used this to build a picture of Erin sending the health department on a wild goose chase — and as the story kept shifting, the goose kept moving. All the while, Don, Gail, Ian, and Heather lay critically ill in hospital. Dying.

Rogers continued her list of deceptions. The disposal of the dehydrator, the concealment of Phone A — her primary device. Phone B, the "dummy phone" — its SIM card inserted only two days before the search — then handed to police as her phone. The multiple factory resets, and the lie about her phone number. Rogers stated that these deceptions were all designed to frustrate the police investigation. "It was all done so police would never see the contents of the accused's mobile phone."

Then Rogers pointed to a fifth deception. One that she said had been delivered in the courtroom itself. The untruthful evidence Erin had given to the jury from the witness box.

Her evidence, Rogers said, seemed to change every time she was asked a question. The foraging story. The gastric bypass appointment. The claim that Simon had accused her of using the dehydrator to poison his parents. Rogers pointed to Erin's remarkable precision on some details — she could recall that 28 April was a Friday — set against her convenient inability to remember others. It simply beggared belief, she said, that a woman with that quality of memory could not recall the suburb where she had purchased dried mushrooms just a couple of months earlier.

When it came to the inconsistencies, Rogers said, the accused simply ignored them, said she couldn't remember, or accused witnesses of being wrong — including her own children.

"Erin Patterson told so many lies it's hard to keep track of them," she said. "She has told lies upon lies because she knew the truth would implicate her."

Rogers reminded the jury that Erin had told them the children ate the leftover steak the night after the lunch. She asked why a mother who knew her guests were in hospital — who, by her own son's account, thought the lunch may have been the cause of their hospitalisation — would then feed those same leftovers to her children.

She wouldn't.

Rogers said there was no doubt that the children did have steak, beans, and mashed potatoes that evening, but not the ingredients that had been served at the lunch. And when doctors urged Erin to bring the children to hospital, her reluctance was not a mother's desire to shield them from fear. It was the confidence of a woman who knew they were never in danger.

Rogers drove the point home with the science. Toxicologists at the Victorian Institute of Forensic Medicine had attempted to separate the mushroom paste from the meat during laboratory testing. They could not do it cleanly — death cap toxins were detected in both the paste and the beef. If trained scientists in a controlled laboratory could not fully separate the two, Rogers told the jury, it was impossible that Erin had managed it with a knife at her kitchen bench.

The children were never fed the contaminated leftovers. Erin knew that. It was why she wasn't worried about them.

Rogers told the jury not to let their emotional response dictate their verdict. They must not feel sorry for the accused. They might not want to believe anyone was capable of what Erin had done. They might not understand it. But they should look at the evidence.

She invited them to consider it as a jigsaw puzzle. A single piece might not tell them much. But, assembled together, the picture became clear. Panic did not explain the extensive and prolonged efforts Erin had made to conceal what she had done — particularly when the lives of her lunch guests were at stake.

Rogers finished with a checklist. She told the jury the evidence showed seven things. Erin had prepared and allocated the meal. She was the only person to eat it without falling seriously ill. She knew how to use the iNaturalist website to find death cap mushrooms in her local area. Cell tower data was consistent with her visiting those areas and remaining long enough to forage. There were remnants of death cap mushrooms in her dehydrator. She had gone to extraordinary lengths to conceal her primary phone from police. And she had told lie after lie after lie.

"When you consider all of the evidence in combination," Rogers said, "you will be satisfied that the accused deliberately sourced death caps and deliberately served death caps."

There was no reasonable alternative explanation. She asked the jury to find Erin guilty on all counts.

Mandy rose. He took his time.

He walked around to the space near the front of the court and began by acknowledging the grief in the room. The victims were good and kind people. Their families were still grieving. It was natural, he said, for the jurors to be moved by that. But he warned them they must "fiercely guard" against the impulse to punish. Sympathy was human. But this was a courtroom, not a chapel. They must use their heads, not their hearts.

Yes. His client was a liar. He didn't shy away from it. "She's not on trial for being a liar," he said. She had told lies, admitted them, and explained them. But a liar is not necessarily a murderer.

He told the jury the case came down to two simple issues. Was there a reasonable possibility that death cap mushrooms had ended up in the meal accidentally? And was there a reasonable possibility that Erin did not intend to kill or cause serious injury? If either was a reasonable possibility, the law required them to acquit.

"If either of those is a reasonable possibility... You find her not guilty. Because that's the law."

He moved to motive. Or rather, the absence of one. The prosecution, he reminded the jury, had conceded they could not prove why Erin had done this. Mandy went further. He argued there was not merely an absence of motive but there was what he called an "anti-motive" — positive evidence that Erin had every reason to keep these people alive. Don tutored her son in maths. They built rockets together. Don and Gail were active, loving grandparents. Erin had a big, beautiful house, financial stability, sole custody of her children, and was looking forward to returning to study.

"She had a motive to keep these people in her world," Mandy said. "Why would she take wonderful, active, loving grandparents away from her own children?"

He reminded the jury that the prosecution had argued Erin had also prepared a poisoned parcel for Simon, in case he changed his mind and attended. If that was true, she was planning to kill her children's father, their grandparents, and their great-uncle and great-aunt — all in a single afternoon.

There was, he told the jury, "no possible prospect" she wanted to "destroy her whole world" and "her whole life."

He listed what he called four "ridiculous" propositions from the prosecution. That Erin would murder without any motive. That she used the cancer lie to lure her guests to the table. That she expected them to take her medical secrets to the grave. And that she would have committed the crime knowing that, as the cook, she would be the first person investigators looked at.

An intelligent person, he argued, would know that if you poison a meal, the meal would be under suspicion and the focus would fall on the cook "very, very quickly."

On the cancer lie, Mandy made a point that the prosecution had not addressed. Erin's announcement came after the meal was eaten, not before. If the cancer story was a ruse to get her guests to the table, it was a redundant one — they had already consumed the food. It served no purpose as a lure if it was delivered after the fact.

On the prosecution's theory, he said, Erin woke up that morning and thought "today's the day" — then pushed ahead regardless. In her own home. With a lavish meal. For guests who everyone knew were coming.

It wasn't a secret. It was all out in the open.

If Erin had been planning murder since April 2023, Mandy argued, she would not have bought the dehydrator in her own name, with her own credit card, from a local store. She would not have photographed mushrooms on its trays. She would not have shared those photographs in a Facebook chat. And she would not have waited months to dispose of it.

"But Erin Patterson did the opposite of all those things because she didn't plan it," he said. "She never planned to kill anyone."

He turned to the plates. He called the evidence "colourful" — adding that he didn't intend the pun. But his argument was sharp.

If the prosecution was right that there were five poisoned parcels and one clean one, the logical way for the cook to keep track of the safe serve was to mark the pastry before it went into the oven. "Easy to do," he said. "In which case, you would not need different coloured plates."

Ian, he said, "had to be wrong." He was "honestly mistaken."

Mandy pointed to the contradictions regarding the plates. Simon had told the court Erin didn't own a matching set. Ben described the plates as "plain white." Kate recalled "a black-and-red one" and "some white ones." No grey plates were found during the police search of her home. It made perfect sense, Mandy argued, for guests picking up plates from a mismatched collection to gravitate toward the ones that most closely matched — creating the impression that the plates had been deliberately divided when they never were.

He turned to the aftermath. The dehydrator disposal. The phone resets. The lies to police. All of it, he argued, was panic. Not the calculated cover-up of a murderer, but the desperate flailing of a woman confronted by the terrible realisation that her actions had caused the illness of people she loved.

He also turned the prosecution's own medical evidence against them. Rogers, he said, had relied on Erin's elevated fibrinogen as a sign of psychological stress — of panic, not poisoning. But Mandy reminded the jury that Professor Bersten's actual evidence was that Erin's medical records were consistent with physical stress caused by a diarrhoeal illness. He said this supported Erin's account, not the prosecution's.

He pointed out that Erin had directed police to the

leftovers in the bin without hesitation. A guilty person would have concealed them.

"She must have been confident that there was no poison in them to do that," he said.

He challenged the prosecution's evidence on the phones. If Erin's intention was to conceal Phone A, why not just take it to the tip? "It could have been done at any time." The fact that she continued to use it after the lunch was more consistent with her account than with the prosecution's theory.

He also challenged the cell tower evidence Rogers had relied on to suggest Erin drove towards Outtrim after leaving the hospital. The data showed her phone had connected to the Outtrim cell tower for less than three minutes — hardly consistent, he said, with the prosecution's theory of a deliberate drive along the Bass Highway.

He took on the witnesses. People, he said, hold "imperfect and honestly mistaken memories." He reminded the jury that Erin had been answering questions from many different people in the days after the lunch. She was under enormous pressure. Minor variations in her account were absolutely inevitable in these circumstances. He singled out nurse Kylie Ashton's evidence, questioning whether her recollection of specific conversations — months after they occurred, in a busy emergency department — could be relied upon with the certainty the prosecution demanded.

He addressed Erin's decision to testify. She didn't have to. The law protected her right to remain silent.

"When she chose to testify, she made that decision as an innocent person," he said.

Her manner in the witness box had been "careful, even pedantic.... You would not have had the impression that she was trying to charm you or persuade you," he told the jury. "She was just going about the job she had."

She told the truth even when it was "deeply embarrassing" — her bulimia, her weight, her loneliness. She admitted her lies. And after what Mandy described as the most "intense surgical examination of someone's account" he could imagine, her account had remained "coherent and consistent day after day."

His client, he declared, had come out of five days of cross-examination "unscathed."

He borrowed Rogers' jigsaw metaphor and turned it back on her. "You can't force jigsaw pieces together," he said. "Jigsaw pieces only fit one way, but evidence can be broken down many ways. It often has multiple reasonable interpretations."

The prosecution, he argued, had worked backwards from assumed guilt, cherry-picking the evidence that supported their theory and ignoring what didn't fit. The jury could not fill gaps with speculation.

"You can only act on the evidence."

He finished where he had started. With the law.

He walked the jury through the standard of proof, step by step. "If you think that it's possible that Erin deliberately poisoned the meal, you must find her not guilty. If you think that maybe she deliberately poisoned the meal, you must find her not guilty. If you think that she probably deliberately poisoned the meal, you must find her not guilty."

He repeated the formulation for intention, and again for the attempted murder of Ian.

Then he said, "Our submission is that the prosecution case cannot get over that high bar of beyond a reasonable doubt."

It had taken him three days to deliver his closing address.

He thanked the jury and took his seat.

Justice Beale then delivered his charge — his final instructions to the jury. He summarised the evidence, explained the legal principles, and outlined the issues they would need to resolve. This took four days.

He started with the fundamentals. Erin was presumed innocent. The burden of proof rested entirely on the prosecution. "This is a court of law," he said, "not a court of morals."

The fact that Erin had cooked the fatal meal did not, on its own, make her a murderer. "The issue is not whether she is in some sense responsible for the tragic consequences of the lunch, but whether the prosecution has proved beyond a reasonable doubt that she is criminally responsible."

The fact that she had admitted to telling lies and concealing evidence should not lead them to convict on that basis alone. But neither should they ignore those lies. If they found she had lied about one matter, they could use that finding to help assess whether she had been truthful about others.

"That is not to say just because you find that the accused lied about one matter, you must also find that she's been lying about everything else."

He acknowledged the emotional weight of what the jury had sat through. "I'm not asking you to be inhuman," he said. "None of us are robots." It was natural to feel for the Patterson and Wilkinson families, given what had befallen them. But sympathy could not cloud their judgement. Nor could it fuel the desire to punish.

He noted potential good character evidence that indicated that Erin had been a good daughter-in-law, a good mother, and generous with her family. The jury could use that when assessing the likelihood she had committed the offences. But, he cautioned, "a person who has previously been of good character can still commit a crime for the first time."

He warned the jury about the influence of the media. "No one in the media, in the public, in your workplace or in your homes has sat in that jury box throughout the trial seeing and hearing all the witnesses, mostly in person," he said. "You, and you alone, are best placed to decide whether the prosecution has proven their case beyond a reasonable doubt. No one else."

As Mandy had previously done, Beale reminded them that Erin had not been required to give evidence. She had chosen to.

He explained four possible paths in their decision making process. If they believed her evidence was true, they must acquit. If they were not sure it was true but thought it might be, they must also acquit. If they merely preferred the prosecution's case to hers, that too was not enough — they must acquit. Only if they rejected her evidence and were satisfied beyond a reasonable doubt could they convict.

He set out the six issues the jury would need to resolve. Whether Erin had good reasons not to kill her lunch guests. Whether she had foraged for mushrooms. Why she had cooked individual beef Wellingtons rather than the log the recipe called for. Whether she had served the meal on different coloured plates and, if so, why. Whether the plates had been allocated deliberately. And whether she had engaged in incriminating conduct after the lunch.

On the individual portions, Beale noted that the prosecution argued Erin had deviated from the recipe because individual servings were critical to maintaining control over which parcels contained death caps. The defence, he observed, had not addressed this point in their closing.

On the cell tower evidence, he gave the jury a specific and important limitation. Dr Sorell's data showed "possible visits" to Loch and Outtrim. "You may not use it as evidence that she actually visited those postcodes," Beale directed.

The fourteen jurors were then balloted down to twelve — their names drawn at random to determine who would deliberate. Beale thanked the two who were excused, telling them he didn't know whether they would feel relieved or frustrated, but that they had made an important contribution to the administration of justice. Seven men and five women remained. Their verdict must be unanimous — all twelve must agree on each of the four charges. "Don't get into little groups and have discussions about the case," he told them.

A couple of days earlier, to lighten the mood after a tense day of testimony, Beale had offered the jury some reassurance. "You don't need to bring your toothbrush tomorrow," he told them. They had laughed.

They needed their toothbrushes now. They would be sequestered. Bussed to undisclosed accommodation. Phones surrendered. Cut off from newspapers, radio and television until they reached their verdicts.

The jury retired to deliberate shortly after 1 p.m. on Monday 30 June.

45 THE VERDICT

7 JULY WAS A COLD, but sunny, Monday. After thirty hours of deliberation over six and a half days, a verdict had been reached.

Many of the media were caught off guard. It was lunchtime. The coffee shops and cafes within walking range of the Morwell Court complex were crowded. Lunch chatter was suddenly replaced by phones ringing and text messages pinging.

Chairs scraped loudly as many diners, seemingly in unison, abandoned half-consumed meals to scramble back to the court complex. Some hadn't even paid. That could come later.

Ian was there, as he had been most days of the trial. Supported by family, he was a dignified, quiet presence. Simon did not attend.

The media presence was overwhelming. Outside the courthouse, a sea of cameras had assembled at the main entrance. Tripods, boom microphones, and satellite trucks lined the footpath. Reporters adjusted earpieces and checked angles. The Latrobe Valley Express — the local paper that had covered school fetes and council meetings in Morwell for decades — was pressing shoulders with the BBC and crews from as far away as the United States and the Middle East.

Apart from her legal team and one friend from her online community, Erin had no family or friends in court. This had been the case throughout the trial. She was largely alone. A curiosity for the media and attending members of the public.

Mandy and Stafford were in court to hear the verdict. Warren and Lenthall represented the prosecution.

The female jury foreperson stood and read the verdicts.

"Guilty." "Guilty." "Guilty." "Guilty."

Four times.

As she read, a number of people in the gallery quietly shed tears. Erin gave nothing away. She sat stone-faced and impassive, her eyes blinking rapidly — the same involuntary response she had displayed in her police interview, on her driveway, and in the witness box.

In the lead-up to the verdict, it was rumoured that Erin was confident of an acquittal. A former Dame Phyllis Frost inmate was quoted as saying Erin was positive she would be found not guilty. She was quoted as saying that "they" didn't have the evidence to convict her. It's not known whether she actually said this, or whether it was just gossip dressed up for the papers.

But the black plastic screens were telling.

Someone, on Erin's behalf, had erected large black plastic screens around the entirety of the balconies and carport of her Leongatha home. If she were found not guilty, the screens would allow her to move from her car to her home without the prying cameras of the media getting a shot of her.

After the verdicts were announced, Beale offered sincere thanks to the jurors, praising their excellent service. He noted how they had stayed upbeat even as the trial stretched on. It had been far longer and more complex than expected. A forty-day trial. More than fifty witnesses. Eight days of testimony from the accused alone. Thirty hours of jury deliberation across six and a half days. He granted each of them dispensation from jury service for fifteen years.

The jury filed out.

Erin's lone supporter, Ali — one of the women from her online friend group — left court wearing sunglasses, tear-stained eyes hidden behind the dark lenses. As she made her way through the media pack, microphones and cameras were thrust toward her.

"Ali, she said she would see you soon. Were you hoping to see her?"

"I will see her," she replied.

The questions kept coming.

"Was there confidence she would walk? Those tarps went up at her house."

Ali said nothing. She continued down the courthouse steps. A reporter hurried beside her.

"When you say you will see her again, are you confident she will appeal this verdict?"

"Was Erin confident she would walk today?"

She kept moving. The questions followed.

"I don't know. I don't know."

"How do you think she was feeling in that moment?"

"I don't know."

Now on the street. The media still in pursuit.

"What do you think she would want to say to the families of those who lost their lives?"

With a heavy sigh, Ali paused, "Could I just get to my car, guys?"

She looked tired. Emotional. Done.

As they stepped out of the court and started down the stairs, Mandy and the defence team were also mobbed by the media. Dressed in their formal courtroom attire, they pushed through the crowd without a word.

The following morning, a message appeared on the noticeboard outside the Korumburra Baptist Church. Attributed to the church's leadership team, it paid quiet tribute to Heather, Don, and Gail, and thanked the community for its support through what it called a "long journey." The families asked for privacy. The church asked the same of its congregation. There were no cameras. No microphones. Just a piece of paper pinned to a board outside a butter-yellow weatherboard church on a hill.

Somewhere in Leongatha, someone took down the black plastic screens from a house on a dirt road.

Three weeks later, the Supreme Court made an order barring Erin from selling that house. The order was sought to preserve the property against any future claims for compensation or restitution by the families of her victims. The home she had built as her forever home — the one she had hoped her children and grandchildren would return to — was now frozen by court order, an asset held in legal limbo.

46 PLEA HEARING

ERIN'S PLEA, or pre-sentencing, hearing, was held in the Supreme Court in Melbourne on 25 August 2025. The court at Morwell, where the trial was held, was undergoing maintenance, so proceedings moved to Melbourne.

As usual, the courtroom was filled to capacity. As he had most days of the trial, Ian Wilkinson came. He was supported by his family — over twenty members of the extended Wilkinson and Patterson families attended.

Erin was transferred from Dame Phyllis Frost and escorted by prison guards. She wore loose black pants, a baggy light brown cardigan, and a paisley shirt, with sandals but no socks. Her hair was tied back, but still looked messy. Her face was drawn. She maintained an emotionless expression as she was led into court, and for much of what followed.

Erin was now a convicted murderer — three counts of murder and one count of attempted murder. Beale had to determine an appropriate sentence. The purpose of the plea hearing is to assist the judge in this regard. It is also an opportunity for victims and their loved ones to share, in their own words, how the crimes have affected them. In the Australian legal system, victim impact statements are taken into consideration by the judge when determining the sentence.

Plea hearings follow a set structure. The court hears victim impact statements first. The defence presents any mitigating factors and their case for leniency. The prosecution then delivers arguments setting out what they think the sentence should be, and why.

The victim impact statements came first. Prosecutor Jane Warren had flagged the likelihood of them occupying the majority of the day. Twenty-eight statements had been submitted in total. Seven were to be read aloud in court. The rest were retained by Justice Beale to read in private.

Of those read in court, Erin had to sit and hear every word.

Ian Wilkinson was the first to address the court.

He stood with his back to Erin, facing the judge, his hands shaking. His voice broke as he described Heather — beautiful, brave, generous, wise, and, simply, he said, a delightful person. Her greatest achievement, he told the court, was their children. He spoke of the silence that had settled into their home since her death, a silence that never stopped reminding him she was gone. He felt, he said, only half alive without her.

He spoke too of Don and Gail, of their close bond of fifty years. Three of the most significant people in his life, gone in the same week. He described the physical toll the poisoning had taken on his body: reduced kidney function, ongoing respiratory difficulties, and a fatigue that had become his permanent companion. He spoke of the practical weight of grief — tying up Heather's affairs alone, navigating a world without her counsel.

And then, quietly, Ian Wilkinson did something that stopped the courtroom.

He offered Erin Patterson his forgiveness. Not for what she had done to others — he was careful to say he had no right to speak on their behalf — but for the harm she had done to him. He sought justice for the murders of Heather, Don, and Gail. But for himself, he chose a different path. "I am no longer Erin Patterson's victim," he said, "and she has become the victim of my kindness." He hoped she would use her time in prison wisely and become a better person.

It was an act of extraordinary grace from a man who had every reason to offer none.

Ruth, Ian and Heather's daughter, followed her father to the stand. "Where do you start?" Her voice was barely steady. She told the court that her family had been handed a lifetime of carrying what she called "this unimaginable horror".

She remembered her mother as one of her closest friends — a guide, a comfort, a source of constant and selfless love. She missed her daily, she said. Life was less bright without her. The bond between the Wilkinson and Patterson families had been close and long; they had always tried, as a family, to show love, to extend empathy, to see the best in people. Ruth said she was distraught to know that these were precisely the qualities Erin had used to draw her loved ones to their deaths.

She reflected on the days that followed the lunch — the hospital vigils, the helplessness, the watching. She noted that there had been moments when Erin might have intervened, might have said something that could have changed the outcome, and had chosen not to. "The following days are in stark contrast," Ruth said. "The events we witnessed in hospital felt like an endless nightmare, and now we have heard in court how seemingly normal life continued for the offender."

Throughout her statement, Ruth referred to Erin not by name, but as "the offender." It was a deliberate choice, and it landed as one.

The intense public scrutiny, she said, had left her family second-guessing every word, uncertain who they could trust. "It is particularly revolting," she told the court, "to experience our family's tragedy being turned into entertainment for the masses."

Other family members followed.

Prosecutor Nanette Rogers read Lyn's statement — Heather and Gail's sister — on her behalf. Lyn reflected on the loss of ordinary family moments. She was supposed to buy a chocolate éclair for Don's birthday. "I cried instead."

Colin, Don's brother, had his statement read to the court. He spoke of Don's quiet, steady role in caring for their elderly mother.

Tim, Don and Gail's nephew, described the anxiety that had become part of his daily life since losing his loved ones. He read excerpts from his diary.

Don's mother — one hundred years old — also gave a statement, read on her behalf. She had outlived her son. She reflected on what good people Don and Gail had been, and said they did not deserve the fate they were given. She asked God for help in their grief. There was nothing more that needed to be said.

Simon did not attend. His statement was read to the court. He wrote of his sadness at the loss of his parents and his aunt. He wrote of his children — deprived of their grandparents, and of a normal family life, saddled with the knowledge that their mother had murdered their grandparents. "They have been robbed of hope," he wrote. He described the community rallying around his family, the police, the medical professionals — set against that, the intrusion of strangers, of media. Notebooks banged against windows. Cameras at his door. People skulking away before police arrived. His children had lived through all of it. He shared his hope that the intrusion would eventually subside.

The details in each statement differed. The loss was the same. Loved ones who had been central to their lives. A deep and lasting sense of injustice. Anxiety that had become ordinary. Nightmares that had replaced what normal once felt like. A family robbed of years, of Christmases, of milestones, of the quiet, unremarkable moments that only become precious once they are no longer possible. Erin had inflicted deep wounds to the Wilkinson and Patterson families. Something they never asked for. Nor deserved.

It was almost 11:30 a.m. The victim impact statements were over. Justice Beale called a short break.

When the court resumed, Jennifer Hosking from Corrections Victoria's Sentence Management Division appeared via video link. She confirmed that Erin was classified as a major offender due to the media attention surrounding the case, and described in detail the restrictive conditions of the Gordon Unit.

Erin's barrister, Colin Mandy, rose. He asked whether Erin might eventually be moved to the Murray Unit — also within Dame Phyllis Frost's protection wing, but considerably less restrictive. Hosking replied that Erin's arrangements were flexible and subject to review. Mandy pressed further, seeking a commitment on when, or whether, Erin might ever leave the isolated Gordon Unit. Hosking was unable to give one.

Through his questioning, Mandy built a picture of what Erin's daily life looked like. Twenty-two hours a day in her cell. A tiny concrete exercise yard. No social contact with other prisoners. Limited access to the gym, library, and chaplaincy service. It was, by any measure, a hard and isolating existence.

Mandy then began his formal plea. He acknowledged the gravity of the offences Erin had been convicted of. His focus, however, was on Erin's prison conditions. He argued that their severity should weigh on the sentence. His client, he said, would always be at risk from other prisoners. Thus, the draconian protective custody arrangements she was held under showed no sign of ending. He said this represented a heavier burden than most prisoners carried. He also raised the possibility that Erin may have Asperger's syndrome and anxiety, conditions that would make her time in prison harder still. He concluded by requesting that a non-parole period be set. Whatever the length of the sentence, he argued, Erin should be given some hope of eventual release.

Jane Warren then rose for the prosecution.

She argued for the maximum penalty. The aggravating factors were significant and numerous. Erin had clearly formed a deadly intent, had used poison as her weapon, had shown an absolute absence of remorse, and had taken elaborate steps to cover her tracks. Warren pointed to the sequence of events in April 2023: the dehydrator purchased within hours of Erin's phone pinging near the death cap mushroom sightings at Loch and Outtrim. The photos of dehydrated mushrooms were saved to her devices in the weeks that followed. This was not a spontaneous act. It was premeditated, methodical, and calculated — the planning having begun at least three months before the lunch. The invitation itself, issued two weeks prior, was part of that plan.

Erin should receive life in prison with no possibility of parole. No opportunity for release. Life, in this case, Warren argued, should mean life.

She then turned to Mandy's claims regarding Asperger's and anxiety. Warren took pointed exception to their use as mitigating factors. There was no medical diagnosis. No supporting report from a medical practitioner. This had come from Erin herself — a self-admitted liar.

Justice Beale weighed in. "She doesn't have a lot of credibility."

Warren conceded that Erin's prison conditions were a relevant consideration. She noted, however, that there was nothing saying Erin would remain in protective custody for her entire sentence. On this point, Justice Beale was less equivocal. He disagreed.

The hearing concluded with Justice Beale setting 8 September as the date he would deliver his sentence.

47 SENTENCING

JUSTICE BEALE DELIVERED Erin's sentence on Monday 8 September 2025. They were back in the same building and the same court as the plea hearing — Court Four of the Victorian Supreme Court in Williams Street, Melbourne.

The hype that had surrounded the trial had not dissipated. Outside the court, a heavy media presence had established itself, and a long queue of people — members of the public, patiently waiting on a cool spring morning — hoped to secure a seat to hear Justice Beale pass sentence. Inside, the court was filled to capacity. Thousands more watched live online.

Erin arrived via a white prison van. The suppression order her legal team had secured during the trial — preventing media from publishing images of her as a prisoner — had expired upon her conviction. As prison officers assisted her out of the back, cameras surged forward. Photographers jostled for position, lenses trained on the van doors before she had even stepped down. She emerged handcuffed, with a fixed, unsmiling look on her face. She looked up toward the sky, before stepping down from the van. Her lips were pressed shut. She was wearing the same outfit as she had at the plea hearing — a loose brown jacket with a camel-coloured cardigan and an untucked paisley shirt underneath. She had a pair of reading glasses perched on her nose. Her hair was loose, with a hint of grey roots visible. Shutters clicked in rapid bursts as prison guards flanked her and escorted her into court. For the first time, the media had the images they had been denied for months.

In court she sat rigid, blinking rapidly.

The sentencing was live streamed via the court's official YouTube page, the camera trained on Justice Beale alone. It was unprecedented. Beale explained his reasoning: "Given the intense public interest in the case, the broadcast will provide an opportunity to inform the public of the reasons for the sentence promptly and completely."

At 9:31 a.m., he began reading from his Sentencing Remarks.

He reiterated the jury's finding. Guilty of three counts of murder, and one of attempted murder. He noted that the prosecution had not submitted a motive for Erin's actions, and was not required to — it was not a legal requirement. The jury had found her guilty, and he was not going to speculate. Dryly, he observed that, "some murders occur for no apparent reason. The motives for such murders may only ever be known to the offenders."

The prosecution had submitted, and the defence conceded, that Erin's offending fell into the worst category — that the maximum penalties were appropriate for her crimes. On that, there was no contest. The question Justice Beale had to decide was whether Erin should receive a non-parole period. Whether she should ever be given the opportunity to leave prison alive.

He summarised the positions of both the prosecution and defence as presented at the plea hearing. The prosecution argued she should not. They submitted that no non-parole period should be fixed — that Erin should remain in prison until she died, with no possibility of parole. Her counsel challenged that position on one specific ground: the conditions of her imprisonment. That was the dispute Justice Beale had to resolve, and it was the lens through which everything that followed was focused.

He moved to the circumstances of the offences, and he was methodical. He pointed out she had been scathing in messages that derided Simon and his family — the "this family, I swear to fucking god" and "lost cause" messages. He noted she had accused Simon of gaslighting her, and his parents of using "weasel words."

He spoke of her planning: her familiarity with the iNaturalist website, which she had used to locate death cap mushroom sightings, and her purchase of a dehydrator, which had enabled her to preserve the mushrooms before incorporating them into the individual beef Wellingtons she served to her guests. He found that she had fabricated a cancer diagnosis to ensure her victims attended the lunch. He made a specific finding that she had served her guests from plates different to her own, and had subsequently disposed of those plates.

"I am satisfied that by July 16, 2023, when you unusually invited Simon, his parents, and aunt and uncle to a lunch without the children to discuss your non-existent medical issue, you did so with the intention of killing them all."

He highlighted the contrast of the day after the lunch — Erin taking a two-hour car journey with the children while her guests were fighting for their lives in hospital. Her reluctance to seek treatment when she finally presented to hospital. Her story about the fictitious Asian grocery store somewhere in Melbourne. The presence of death cap mushrooms in the meal was no accident. He observed that, when she realised the lie wouldn't hold — death cap mushrooms can't be commercially cultivated — she changed tack. "You concocted the story you told the jury about foraged mushrooms accidentally ending up in the beef Wellingtons."

He listed her many lies and her subsequent attempts to conceal her crimes — the discarded plates, the shifting accounts of the mushrooms' origin, the phones. He spoke of her attempts to destroy evidence, including the trip to the Koonwarra Transfer Station to dispose of the dehydrator.

He moved to her callous disregard for her victims — her refusal to offer any meaningful assistance to medical staff as her elderly guests continued to deteriorate. They suffered a protracted and violent illness while Erin did nothing. "The prosecution submitted that I should infer from your pitiless behaviour that the intention to kill was ongoing, and that this constitutes an additional aggravating circumstance. I accept that submission."

He saved the most serious aggravating factor for last.

"Your offending involved an enormous betrayal of trust."

Erin responded by closing her eyes — shutting his words out. For the majority of the remaining hearing, she kept them closed.

He continued.

"Your victims were all your relatives by marriage. More than that, they had all been good to you and your children over many years, as you acknowledged in your testimony. You cut short three lives and caused lasting damage to Ian Wilkinson's health. You inflicted untold suffering on your own children, whom you robbed of their beloved grandparents."

He noted her lack of contrition — "You maintain your innocence. In other words, there is no evidence of remorse."

He turned to the victim impact statements. He observed that Erin's crimes had irrevocably affected four generations of the Wilkinson and Patterson families — the emotional toll, their struggle to manage work and studies, and the additional financial burdens. A word that appeared again and again in the statements, Justice Beale noted, was "senseless." He noted that her "failure to exhibit any remorse pours salt into the victims' wounds." He pointed to Ian Wilkinson's victim impact statement, in which Ian had expressed forgiveness. "His offer of forgiveness presents you with an opportunity. You would do well to embrace it in the manner he suggests."

He had no hesitation in finding that Erin's offending fell into the worst category for the offences of murder and attempted murder.

He then turned to Erin's personal circumstances and character. The information provided by her legal counsel about her personal history was minimal. Her counsel had simply relied on the evidence she had given during her trial testimony. There were no psychiatric or psychological reports. No references from character witnesses. No doubt, Beale observed, that approach to the plea hearing was based on her instructions — but it meant the account he was able to give of her personal history was limited.

Her counsel had claimed she had Asperger's syndrome. The claim was based on her own self-report to various people. There was no expert evidence to support it. Given her acknowledged credibility problem — she had, on her own admission, told many lies — Beale was not willing to accept the claim in the absence of corroborating expert evidence.

He turned to the conditions of her imprisonment. Isolation, no contact with other prisoners, meals delivered through a flap without human interaction, limited access to the library, and a requirement that she be escorted by two prison guards wherever she went — meaning that if they were occupied, she went nowhere.

He observed the unprecedented media interest in the case. He said Erin was likely to remain a notorious prisoner for many years to come — and with that notoriety, at continuing risk from other prisoners.

Erin opened her eyes. She glared at the assembled media.

On the question of a non-parole period, he observed that sentencing case law establishes that harsher than normal conditions of imprisonment will, as a general rule, warrant some mitigation of penalty. "The harsh prison conditions that you have experienced already and the likely prospect of solitary confinement for the foreseeable future are important and weighty considerations which should count for something in the sentencing exercise. In my view, the only scope for making them count is by the fixing of a non-parole period."

He was careful to say this was not intended to diminish the gravity of her crimes. Her total effective sentence would be life imprisonment. The period during which she would be ineligible for parole would be a very substantial one. And he noted, pointedly, that parole is not automatic.

It was time.

He looked directly at Erin. "Please stand."

Her chair creaked as she rose.

Twenty-five years for the attempted murder of Ian. A life sentence for each of the three murders. Concurrent sentences. Life in prison, with a non-parole period of thirty-three years. He gave her credit for the 676 days she had served of pre-sentence detention. The arithmetic of that non-parole period, taken from her credited start date, placed her earliest possible application for parole at around October 2056. She would be eighty-two years old. And even then, release would not be guaranteed.

He had spoken for forty-six minutes.

"Would you please remove Ms Patterson?"

Erin left just as she had arrived — stone-faced. As she was led from the court, she did something odd. She tapped twice on the media bench. Then she was gone.

It was just on dusk when the prison van left the court

complex and began its journey back to Dame Phyllis Frost Centre. Media, rugged up in jumpers and jackets, ran alongside the van, lifting cameras to the high van windows. Trying to get footage and photos of Erin.

As the courtroom emptied, media crews jostled for position outside the courthouse entrance. Cameras swung toward every door. Microphones were held aloft, ready for whoever emerged first.

Ian stepped outside the Supreme Court into the weak sunshine.

He stopped briefly on the steps to address the assembled media. His hands trembled, shaking the notes he was holding, and his voice quavered slightly as he began. He said he would keep his remarks brief — he wanted to give some well-earned thanks. "Firstly, to the Victoria Police, in particular the Homicide Squad and the team led by Detective Stephen Eppingstall. They made a professional, efficient, and effective investigation into what happened at the lunch." He offered thanks to the prosecution team, the hospital staff who had cared for him and his family members, and his local community for their support over the prior two years. Then he folded his notes and stepped down. The media gave Ian the respect he deserved, stepping aside to let him pass. A couple murmured, "Thank you, Ian." None tried to bombard him with questions.

Detective Inspector Thomas also stopped briefly on the steps of the court. He implored the media not to forget the human tragedy. The people who had died.

Three months later, Beale retired from the bench. The Patterson case had been his last major trial.

ACT V — THE AFTERMATH

48 LIFE IN PRISON

ERIN HAS ALWAYS STRUGGLED with her incarceration. After her arrest, she was denied bail, so she has remained in custody since 2 November 2023. Since then, she has been held at the Dame Phyllis Frost Centre, a maximum-security women's prison in the Melbourne suburb of Ravenhall.

Designed to house 538 female prisoners, the prison has two distinct populations: mainstream and protection. Mainstream prisoners are housed in self-contained units of up to ten women. Each unit has its own kitchen and dining facilities. Prisoners cook their own meals, do their own washing, ironing, and housework, and move freely among their unit-mates. They have reasonable outdoor time and access to a prison library, with generous visiting hours throughout the week.

Protection prisoners are held in either the Murray or Gordon units, with the Gordon being the more restrictive of the two.

From her first night in custody, Erin was placed in the

Gordon Unit. This enabled prison authorities to keep a close eye on her as she settled in. After six weeks, she was moved to the Murray Unit, which allowed some interaction with other inmates. It was here that she found the knitting circle — where inmates are permitted to use knitting needles under close supervision. It was here, too, that she earned a reputation for complaints. The temperature of her cell. The noise from other inmates. Other prisoners heckled her regularly. "Have you got any mushrooms?" was a favourite.

But the Murray Unit didn't last. Over the following months, she was shifted back and forth — briefly returned to Gordon in March 2024, then back to Murray, before being placed in the Gordon Unit permanently in June 2024. A prison source said that safety concerns were the driver. The nature of her crimes — targeting elderly victims — was said to have put her at increased risk of harm from other prisoners.

There were also some unsubstantiated rumours.

A former inmate, who kept a diary during her time at Dame Phyllis Frost, later claimed that, during her time in Murray, Erin had tampered with another prisoner's food. The Department of Justice issued a statement that there was "no evidence to support that there has been any contaminated food or suspected poisonings" at the prison.

Erin's world in the Gordon Unit is very small. She spends between twenty-two and twenty-four hours a day in her cell. She is segregated from other prisoners. Her meals arrive through a trapdoor.

Contact with her children is tightly controlled. She has supervised in-person visits once a month, and is usually permitted Zoom contact with them on Tuesdays and Saturdays — though not if she has had, or is about to have, an in-person visit within a couple of days.

Prison library visits must be coordinated, escorted, and scheduled only when no mainstream prisoners are present. She has designated times she is permitted outside, and even then, it is into a small concrete-walled exercise yard designed to keep her isolated from the rest of the prison population.

During the plea hearing on 25 August 2025, Erin's barrister, Colin Mandy, raised her library access with the court. "Every single Friday, she has said she wants access to the library," he said. "She only has access to the library if no one else is using it, with the result she's had access to the library a handful of times since she's been in the Gordon Unit." She was also unable to access the lounge area or exercise equipment. Mandy warned the court that his client was likely to remain notorious in the prison system and could face "vitriol and animus" from other prisoners for years to come. Movement back into the mainstream prison population may never be safe for her.

Erin's next-door neighbour is convicted terrorist Momena Shoma, a self-described "soldier of Islamic State," who is serving a forty-eight-year sentence. Their only chance for contact comes during brief periods in their small adjoining exercise yards. Despite their proximity, the two women have never spoken.

Erin does have some small comforts — a television, a computer, books, a hair straightener, and crocheting equipment. Gordon Unit prisoners are not permitted knitting needles, so the knitting circle she had been part of in the Murray Unit was no longer an option. A crochet hook is blunt and poses limited risk. It was a practical adjustment rather than a change of craft — though she has taken to crocheting, reportedly even making small handmade gifts for members of her legal team.

Outside Dame Phyllis Frost, the world has moved on. Erin has lost the courtroom platform where her barrister could lodge her various complaints before a judge. All that remains is her appeal, her very small world, and the Dame Phyllis Frost formal grievance process.

49 THE CIRCUS LEAVES TOWN

THIS CASE DREW intense media interest that the communities of Leongatha, Korumburra, and Morwell were wholly unprepared for — not just locally, but nationally and internationally. It started the moment the story broke, and did not let up until after Erin was sentenced.

Within days, journalists and television crews descended on the region, knocking on doors, lingering outside hospitals, trying to find an exclusive angle or a new sound bite. Microphones and cameras were stuck in the face of anyone willing to speak. Strangers wandered into Leongatha shops asking for directions to Erin's house.

When the trial moved to Morwell in April 2025, the circus intensified. Journalists, podcasters, screenwriters, photographers, and true crime buffs flooded the Latrobe Valley. For ten weeks, Morwell was the unlikely centre of national and international attention.

A coffee shop around the corner from the courthouse saw its trade triple. A motel manager described a boom in bookings from journalists and legal teams during what was normally the quietest time of year. One local cafe even chalked up mushroom soup on its specials board.

For the millions who couldn't be there in person, the trial was consumed through their earbuds. At least three network-backed podcasts ran daily episodes from Morwell, including the ABC's *Mushroom Case Daily,* recorded from a makeshift studio in town. The show drew more than half a million listeners monthly. As coverage intensified, speculation also grew about documentary and mini-series projects already in development. The story had become content before it had even finished being told.

On Google Maps, someone posted two fake restaurant listings on her Gibson Street home — "Erin's Mushroom Restaurant" and "Erin's Mushroom Diner."

In a Melbourne laneway near the Queen Victoria Market, a street artist painted a mural of Erin mid-trial, titled "Bon Appétit." Within twenty-four hours of the guilty verdict, the words "GUILTY" were across her face in large red letters.

But not everyone welcomed the attention. The local newsagent in Morwell expressed her hope that the trial wouldn't taint the region's reputation. The Latrobe Valley had already carried the stigma of one notorious case — the death of thirteen-month-old Jaidyn Leskie in 1997. The toddler disappeared from his mother's boyfriend's home near Moe. His body was found six months later in a nearby dam. The boyfriend was charged with murder but acquitted, and the case remains unsolved. The intense media coverage at the time had cast the region in an unflattering light, and locals had long memories.

South Gippsland Shire councillor Nathan Hersey

acknowledged the scale of publicity around Erin's trial had astounded locals, and noted that much of it had been negative. But, he added, anyone who knew Gippsland knew it was a great place with fantastic people.

For the Patterson and Wilkinson families, the relentless media attention was its own kind of injury. The victim impact statements read out during the pre-sentencing hearing bore testimony to that. But their community had been protective, and the families appreciated it. In his statement, Simon noted, "The sensitivity of the local community in relating with our family, including by minimising their communication about us to reporters, has also been amazing."

On the steps of the Supreme Court after sentencing, Ian Wilkinson echoed that sentiment, thanking the people of Leongatha and Korumburra specifically. Their thoughtfulness, he said, had been a great encouragement.

After Erin's sentencing, South Gippsland Mayor John Schelling gave a morning television interview. He expressed sympathy for the families and spoke of his community's relief that the matter was finally concluded. The region, he made clear, did not wish to be defined by what had happened. So many people had descended on the town, he said, but the community wanted to move on. To go back to being dairy farmers.

When it was put to him that local cafes and motels had been doing a roaring trade, he steered back to what mattered — the community had lost some of their own, and now they wished to embrace the families left behind.

The towns would have gladly forgone every extra dollar they made from it. No full cafe or booked-out motel was worth the lives of three of their own. Given the choice, they would have taken back their quiet, unremarkable lives without a moment's hesitation.

The circus finally left town. It was time for the community — and the families — to start to heal.

50 WHAT MOTIVE?

THROUGHOUT THE TRIAL AND BEYOND, motive has been debated across media outlets, forums, and podcasts with an intensity nearing obsession.

Crown Prosecutor Nanette Rogers introduced the language of duality in court: Erin, she told the jury, had two faces — a public one that projected warmth and goodwill toward the Pattersons, and a private one that bristled with contempt. Other than this less-than-flattering commentary on her personality, the prosecution's case didn't touch on motive. It was deliberate. They had suspicions. But suspicions aren't proof. And they had no obligation to establish motive. Under Victorian law, the jury only needed to be satisfied that Erin had intentionally served death cap mushrooms, knowing they were lethal. Not why. The prosecution's case sat on firmer ground for the omission.

In his closing argument, Erin's barrister presented a kind of anti-motive. He argued that Erin had plenty of reasons NOT to kill her lunch guests. Her relationship with Simon's parents was warm and longstanding. Don and Gail were her children's grandparents. Erin was, by any objective measure, financially secure and emotionally stable. She had everything to lose and nothing to gain. The jury heard all of this, but convicted her anyway. The anti-motive argument was a reasonable one to make. It just wasn't persuasive enough.

In his sentencing remarks, Justice Beale was clear. He was not going to speculate on a motive for Erin's crimes. "Only you know why you committed them," he said. "I will not be speculating about that matter."

The public couldn't let it go.

Outside domestic violence, money is very often found to be the motive for the murder of family members. But Erin would not benefit financially from the deaths of her relatives. There was no inheritance to collect. No insurance payout with her named as the beneficiary. No property that would revert to her. Three people died, and Erin was not a single dollar richer for it.

The rupture that seemed to change everything was, on its face, mundane. In 2022, Simon updated his tax return to reflect their separation. The change reduced Erin's family tax benefit payments. Simon said it was an error. Erin didn't believe him. From that point, the warmth that had characterised their post-separation arrangement — shared custody, family holidays, church on Sundays — began to curdle. She stopped attending family events. Her private messages about Simon and his family descended into vitriolic rants: he was a deadbeat, his family a lost cause. When she appealed to Don and Gail to intervene in the dispute, they declined. Her messages to online friends left little room for ambiguity: she felt that was a betrayal. She went into detail about how, if it were Simon's sister having this same issue, they would take her side without hesitation.

A child support dispute does not explain three deaths. It may, however, explain the first crack in what had, until then, been a veneer of family harmony.

The loss of community may be another factor.

Erin had grown up, by her own description, a "fundamental atheist." She converted to Christianity and started attending church regularly after meeting Simon. The Korumburra Baptist Church became the social centre of her and Simon's lives. Her community, her calendar, her sense of belonging. Ian Wilkinson — the man who would survive her lunch and later offer her his forgiveness — was the church's pastor. When their separation became permanent, Erin's place within that world began to feel uncertain. Her messages from this period reflect the dislocation. She complained to multiple people that Simon was pushing her out of his world, cutting her off from his family.

A former housemate was quoted as saying that Erin had been drawn to Simon partly because of the ready-made community that came with him — that beneath her self-sufficient exterior, she was deeply lonely. If that's true, then what Erin lost in the separation was not merely a husband but the entire social world she had built around him, and had converted her deepest beliefs to enter.

The concept of an "injustice collector" has been applied to Erin in podcasts and commentary, and it aligns closely with the definition offered by FBI behavioural analyst Mary Ellen O'Toole in her work on seemingly motiveless crimes. She uses the term to describe a person who accumulates perceived slights — real or imagined — and stores them as evidence of having been wronged. Even minor frustrations are reinterpreted as significant betrayals, and over time, these grievances form a private ledger of injustices. The eventual response, when it comes, is often wildly disproportionate to the original events because it is aimed not at a single slight but at the entire accumulated archive.

If that framework was applied to Erin, several elements documented in the public record take on a different cast. The tax return dispute, the birthday invitation, the school fees, the belief that Don and Gail had sided with Simon — none of these incidents, on their own, would typically provoke more than irritation or hurt feelings. But through the lens of someone inclined to interpret ordinary interpersonal friction as targeted injury, each becomes another entry in a long-running narrative of being mistreated. Seen this way, Erin's motive would not be focused on any single grievance. Rather, it would be the overall emotional weight created by what she may have experienced as a slow death by a thousand cuts.

The timeline bears this out. The tax return change came first — Simon formalising a separation that had existed for seven years but had never been declared. Then the child support assessment: $38 a month, an amount so small it felt like an insult. The birthday lunch invitation that arrived late, or not at all, depending on who you believed. The school fees Simon refused to pay outside the assessed amount. And when

Erin appealed to Don and Gail — people she expected to take her side — they suggested she and Simon pray together. In her private messages, the reaction was immediate, "fuck 'em." Each incident was minor. Each response was not. And by late 2022, the woman who had once described Gail as the best mother-in-law anyone could ask for was telling her online friends that the whole family was a lost cause.

A forensic psychologist, speaking to the media, discussed the profile typical of a poisoner: someone characteristically less confrontational than other violent offenders, prone to expressing aggression indirectly, a meticulous planner who may derive cold satisfaction from the secrecy and control the method provides. It could be argued that Erin's months of preparation — the iNaturalist searches, the dehydrator, the careful individual pastry parcels — make her a good fit for this profile also.

Others have pointed to a pattern of compulsive deception and a need to control the narrative of her own life, stretching back long before the lunch.

In his article, "Anatomy of the Mushroom Murders," British sociologist and author Ellis Cashmore suggested the cause lay in what he described as "weakened social bonds, perceived strains and a slow slide into moral suspension". When considering Erin's circumstances, there may have been the possibility that Simon was moving on, Erin's increasing resentment toward him, and her growing distrust of his extended family. Conditions potentially fertile for a warped sense of revenge. Perhaps.

It is important to note that none of the clinicians or commentators who offered these observations have ever assessed Erin directly. Diagnosis from a distance is a fraught exercise.

Then there were the Facebook and Reddit chat forums.

One theory posited that, unable to lure Simon to a lunch he ultimately declined, she killed his loved ones instead — knowing it would hurt him deeply and permanently. Another focused on the children: possessive of them and determined that they belonged to her alone, she had removed a substantial portion of Simon's family from their lives. A third dispensed with psychology entirely. Out of spite, it said. Simply that.

Then there was the theory that Erin's long immersion in true crime — the podcasts, the books, the forums, the years spent dissecting how killers operated and how they were caught — had given her something dangerous: a belief that she understood the method well enough to execute it, and the investigative process well enough to survive it. It is the least evidenced of all the theories, and perhaps the one that most resists examination. What can be said is that she was meticulous in her planning, and that her meticulous planning ultimately failed her. Her interest in how criminals are caught did not help her avoid getting caught.

Ultimately, though, every theory founders on the same question.

If Simon was the primary target, why did she proceed after he withdrew? He had declined the night before. She knew he would not be there. She could have postponed. She could have cancelled. The people who came to her table that winter afternoon were his elderly parents, his aunt, and his uncle — people who had, by her own admission in court, treated her like one of their own for years. People who had prayed for her. People who had delighted in her children.

Why them? Why then? Why at all?

No profiler has answered this. No psychologist, criminologist, or forensic expert has answered this. The prosecutor and sentencing judge both declined to try to answer it. Whatever the courts ultimately determine, the question of why will also remain untouched by any future proceedings. Courts establish what happened and whether it was proved. They do not resolve what drove a person toward an act that cost three people their lives and shattered four generations of two families.

Perhaps the most haunting possibility is also the simplest: Erin Patterson was a woman who craved connection and community above almost everything else, and who destroyed the very thing she had spent years reaching for. Whether she acted out of cold calculation, wounded fury, or something that resists any clean description, only Erin knows.

And she isn't talking.

THE LEGAL BATTLE is not yet over.

ON 6 OCTOBER 2025, the prosecution filed an appeal, arguing that Erin's sentence was manifestly inadequate. The Crown's position is that Justice Beale should not have set a non-parole period, and that in this case, life should have meant life.

A MONTH LATER, Erin's legal team, now led by barristers Richard Edney and Julian McMahon SC, lodged their own application for leave to appeal her convictions. Their application argues that a substantial miscarriage of justice has occurred. Among the seven grounds they raise are an alleged irregularity during the jury's sequestration — relating to their accommodation arrangements — and an argument that the prosecution's cross-examination of Erin was "unfair and oppressive." The application also challenges the admissibility of key evidence, including the cell tower data, the iNaturalist material, and the Facebook messages. Erin's appeal submission further contends that the trial judge erred in excluding certain evidence that the defence sought to rely on, and alleges the prosecution improperly shifted its position on motive between its opening and closing addresses.

IT IS standard procedure for the Court of Appeal to hear related appeals together, particularly when they involve the same trial and evidence. At the time of this writing, no date has been set.

51 TIMELINE OF KEY EVENTS

- June 2007 — Simon Patterson and Erin Scutter marry.
- November 2015 — Simon and Erin separate permanently.
- October 2021 – May 2023 — Multiple accesses to iNaturalist and poison-related material from Erin's home computers.
- November 2021 – September 2022 — Simon hospitalised three times with food-poisoning - like symptoms.
- 28 May 2022 — Erin's home computer used to search iNaturalist for death cap sightings.
- October 2022 — Tax return issue. Relationship between Erin and Simon deteriorates.
- November – December 2022 — Erin sends hostile messages about Simon and his parents to her online friends.

- February 2023 — Simon confides poisoning suspicions to his general practitioner.
- 18 April 2023 — Christine McKenzie posts death cap sighting in Loch to iNaturalist.
- 28 April 2023 — Erin's phone connects to cell towers in the Loch area. Erin purchases a Sunbeam Food Lab dehydrator.
- 30 April – 4 May 2023 — Erin photographs mushrooms on dehydrator trays. Images saved on Samsung tablet.
- 21 May 2023 — Dr Tom May posts verified death cap sighting at Outtrim to iNaturalist.
- 22 May 2023 — Erin's phone connects to cell towers near Loch and Outtrim.
- 24 June 2023 — Erin hosts Don and Gail to lunch. Children present. Simon declines invitation.
- 28 June – 7 July 2023 — Erin sends messages to Gail falsely representing she has undergone a needle biopsy and MRI.
- 16 July 2023 – Erin invites Don, Gail, Heather, Ian, and Simon to lunch on 29 July, citing important medical news.
- 28 July 2023 — Simon declines lunch invitation by text.
- 29 July 2023 — The fatal lunch. Erin visits Koonwarra Transfer Station less than an hour later. Guests fall ill around midnight.
- 30 July 2023 — All four guests hospitalised. Erin drives to Tyabb for son's flying lesson

(cancelled). Don and Gail transferred to Dandenong Hospital.

- 31 July 2023 — Don and Gail transferred to Austin Hospital. Ian and Heather transferred to Dandenong Hospital. Erin and children hospitalised for observation.
- 1 August 2023 — Ian and Heather transferred to Austin Hospital. Erin and children discharged from Monash.
- 2 August 2023 — Erin factory resets Phone B. Drives to Koonwarra Transfer Station and disposes of the dehydrator. Ignores calls from Department of Health.
- 3 August 2023 — Homicide Squad commences investigation. Erin moves SIM card into Phone B.
- 4 August 2023 — Police recover dehydrator from tip. Gail Patterson and Heather Wilkinson die. Don Patterson receives liver transplant.
- 5 August 2023 — Police execute search warrant at Erin's home. Erin factory resets Phone B and gives it to police. Erin interviewed by police at Wonthaggi Police Station. Don Patterson dies.
- 6 August 2023 — Erin remotely factory resets Phone B while it is in police custody. Victorian health authorities publicly report three deaths from suspected mushroom poisoning.

- 7 August 2023 — Detective Inspector Dean Thomas declares Erin a suspect. Erin confronted by media on her driveway.
- 10 August 2023 — Erin hires criminal lawyer Bill Doogue. Written statement provided to police.
- 14 August 2023 — Ian extubated. Condition improving.
- 21 August 2023 — Ian moved from intensive care to a general ward in Austin Hospital.
- 31 August 2023 — Memorial service for Don and Gail.
- 11 September 2023 — Ian transferred to Heidelberg Repatriation Hospital.
- 19 September 2023 — Ian gives police statement.
- 22 September 2023 — Ian discharged home.
- 24 September 2023 — Skip bin observed in Erin's front yard.
- 4 October 2023 — Memorial service for Heather.
- 2 November 2023 — Police execute second search warrant. Erin arrested and charged with three counts of murder and five counts of attempted murder.
- 3 November 2023 — First court appearance, Latrobe Valley Magistrates' Court.
- 22 April 2024 — Initial committal mention hearing.

- 7 May 2024 — Formal plea of not guilty entered. Erin committed to stand trial. Elects to bypass committal and fast-track to Supreme Court.
- 23 May 2024 — Post-committal directions hearing.
- February 2025 — Pre-trial hearings on admissibility of evidence. Attempted murder charges relating to Simon severed.
- March – April 2025 — Pre-trial rulings delivered.
- 17 April 2025 — Court of Appeal upholds severance ruling.
- 29 April 2025 — Trial begins. Charges relating to Simon discontinued.
- 7 July 2025 — Guilty verdict. All counts.
- 25 August 2025 — Plea (or pre-sentencing) hearing.
- 8 September 2025 — Sentence delivered — life, 33-year non-parole period.
- 6 October 2025 — Prosecution filed an appeal against the sentence.
- 3 November 2025 — Defence lodged an appeal against the convictions

52 PHONES

- **Phone A** — Samsung Galaxy A70, IMEI ending 2137, SIM ending 783 — activated 12 June 2021. Erin's usual or primary phone. Never recovered.
- **Phone B** — Samsung Galaxy A23, IMEI ending 8276, SIM ending 835 — activated 11 July 2023. Handed to police 5 August 2023 as 'her phone'.
- **Black Nokia** — seized during first search 5 August 2023. Described by Erin as "a really old" spare.
- **Phone C** — second Nokia, IMEI ending 2489, SIM ending 783. Carried the 783 SIM from 6 August. Last network activity detected 14 August. Never recovered.

53 KEY PEOPLE

THE LUNCH GUESTS

- **Patterson, Don** — Erin's father-in-law. Retired science teacher. Married to Gail for 50 years. Died 5 August 2023, aged 70.
- **Patterson, Gail** — Erin's mother-in-law. Retired school office administrator. Don's wife. Died 4 August 2023, aged 70.
- **Wilkinson, Heather** — Gail's sister. Retired integration aide and literacy volunteer. Married to Ian. Died 4 August 2023, aged 66.
- **Wilkinson, Ian** — Heather's husband. Pastor of the Korumburra Baptist Church. Sole surviving lunch guest. 70 years old at the time of the lunch.

THE ACCUSED AND IMMEDIATE FAMILY

- **Patterson, Erin** (née Scutter) — Host of the fatal lunch. Simon's estranged wife. Mother of Ben and Kate. Convicted of three counts of murder and one count of attempted murder.
- **Patterson, Simon** — Erin's estranged husband. Don and Gail's son. Civil engineer. The couple separated permanently in November 2015.
- **Patterson, Ben** — Erin and Simon's son. Fourteen at the time of the lunch. Name changed by court order.
- **Patterson, Kate** — Erin and Simon's daughter. Nine at the time of the lunch. Name changed by court order.

EXTENDED FAMILY

- **Anna** — Don and Gail's youngest daughter. Simon's sister. Was previously close to Erin.
- **Ceinwen** — Erin's older sister. Geologist.
- **Colin** — Don's brother. Spoke at Don and Gail's memorial service. Gave a victim impact statement at the plea hearing.
- **David** — Ian and Heather's son. Walked Erin down the aisle at her wedding.
- **Lyn** — Sister of Heather and Gail. The only

surviving sister. Her victim impact statement was read to the court at the plea hearing.

- **Matt** — Don and Gail's oldest son. Simon's brother. Married to Tanya. Erin emailed Matt and Tanya asking them to care for her children if anything happened to her.
- **Ruth** — Ian and Heather's youngest daughter.
- **Scutter, Eitan** — Erin's father. Died 2011.
- **Scutter, Heather** — Erin's mother. Academic at Monash University. Died 2019.
- **Tanya** — Matt's wife. Gave evidence about visiting Erin in hospital and about conversations in the days after the lunch.
- **Tim** — Don and Gail's nephew. Described the anxiety that had become part of his daily life in his victim impact statement.

INVESTIGATION

- **Eppingstall, Stephen** (Detective Leading Senior Constable) — Homicide Squad. Appointed Informant (lead investigator). Conducted Erin's first police interview.
- **Farrell, Luke** (Detective Sergeant) — Homicide Squad. Coordinated the first search of Erin's home on 5 August 2023.
- **Fox-Henry, Shamen** — Senior Digital Forensic Officer, Victoria Police Cybercrime Squad. Examined Erin's seized electronic devices.

- **Geremia, Sonia** — Senior fingerprint specialist, Victoria Police. Matched latent prints on the dehydrator to Erin's left hand.
- **Goodwin, Ben** — Forensic officer, Victoria Police. Examined the dehydrator and extracted seven samples of vegetable matter from its trays.
- **Thomas, Dean** (Detective Inspector) — Head of the Homicide Squad. Fronted two police press conferences. Declared Erin a suspect on 7 August 2023.

MEDICAL PROFESSIONALS

- **Ashton, Kylie** — Director of Nursing, Leongatha Hospital. Attempted to dissuade Erin from leaving the hospital on 31 July.
- **Beer, Dr Brian** — Forensic pathologist. Performed the autopsies on Don, Gail, and Heather. Confirmed death cap poisoning as the cause of death in each case.
- **Bersten, Professor Andrew** — Intensive care specialist. Reviewed Erin's medical records. Found no evidence of cancer diagnosis or acute illness.
- **Douglas, Dr Mark** — Toxicology registrar, Dandenong Hospital. Devised the initial treatment plan for Don. First to conclude *Amanita* poisoning was the likely cause.

- **Foote, Dr Veronica** — Doctor at Leongatha Hospital. Warned Erin it was not safe for her to drive.
- **Ford, Dr Christopher** — Simon's general practitioner. Simon confided his suspicions about Erin's cooking to Ford in February 2023.
- **McDermott, Dr Conor** — Toxicology registrar, Austin Hospital. Phoned Erin on behalf of the Victorian Poisons Information Centre.
- **Morgan, Dr Beth** — Overnight registrar at Dandenong Hospital. Tests she ordered first identified the suspected death cap poisoning.
- **Muldoon, Dr Laura** — Emergency registrar, Monash Medical Centre. Found no clinical or biochemical evidence of *Amanita* poisoning in Erin.
- **Munro, Cindy** (nurse) — Leongatha Hospital. Cared for Ian and Heather. Observed that Erin "didn't look unwell" compared to her other patients.
- **Ruggoo, Dr Varuna** — Doctor at Monash Medical Centre. Confirmed Erin's liver function tests were within normal limits. Deemed her fit for discharge.
- **Shannon, Lisa** (nurse) — After-hours coordinator, Korumburra Hospital. Cared for Don and Gail on the morning of 30 July.

- **Spencer, Eleyne** (paramedic) — Transported Erin from Leongatha to Monash. Described her as "calm and nonchalant."
- **Stuart, Professor Rhonda** — Director of Public Health and Infection Prevention, Monash Health. Spoke to Erin at Monash Hospital about the source of the mushrooms.
- **Warrillow, Professor Stephen** — Director of Intensive Care, Austin Hospital. Treated all four lunch guests. Gave evidence about the progression of their illnesses and deaths.
- **Webster, Dr Chris** — Doctor on duty at Leongatha Hospital on 31 July. First to confront Erin about the mushrooms. Called triple zero when she left after five minutes.

EXPERT WITNESSES

- **Gerostamoulos, Dr Dimitri** — Chief toxicologist, Victorian Institute of Forensic Medicine. Confirmed death cap toxins in the beef Wellington leftovers and dehydrator debris.
- **Lovelock, David** — Diagnostics manager, Agriculture Victoria Research. DNA analysis confirmed death cap mushroom residue in the dehydrator.
- **May, Dr Tom** — Principal Research Scientist in Mycology, Royal Botanic Gardens Victoria. Australia's foremost authority on mushroom

identification. Also posted the Outtrim death cap sighting to iNaturalist.

- **Sorell, Dr Matthew** — Digital forensics and telecommunications specialist. Analysed cell tower data to map the movements of Erin's phone.
- **Truong, Dr Camille** — Mycology research scientist, Royal Botanic Gardens. First mycologist to examine the beef Wellington leftovers. Found field mushrooms but no death cap remnants.

THE BENCH

- **Beale, Justice Christopher** — Supreme Court judge. Presided over the pre-trial hearings, trial, and sentencing.
- **Dixon, Justice Jane** — Supreme Court judge. Ruled that the trial would be held in Morwell rather than Melbourne.
- **Freeman, Judicial Registrar Tim** — Managed case directions in the Supreme Court, including setting the trial date.
- **Walsh, Magistrate Tim** — Presided over Erin's early appearances in the Latrobe Valley Magistrates' Court.
- **Court of Appeal panel — Justices Emerton, Priest, and T Forrest.** Upheld Justice Beale's ruling to sever the indictment, refusing the prosecution's appeal on coincidence evidence.

LEGAL REPRESENTATIVES

- Trial — Prosecution

- **Lenthall, Sarah** — Crown Prosecutor. Junior counsel for the prosecution.
- **Rogers, Dr Nanette SC** — Senior Crown Prosecutor. Led the prosecution.
- **Warren, Jane** — Crown Prosecutor. Junior counsel for the prosecution.

- Trial — Defence

- **Doogue, Bill** — Erin's instructing solicitor. Founder of Doogue + George Defence Lawyers.
- **Mandy, Colin SC** — Senior Counsel. Led Erin's defence at trial.
- **Stafford, Sophie** — Junior counsel for the defence.

- Appeal — Defence

- **Edney, Richard** — Barrister leading Erin's appeal against her convictions.
- **McMahon, Julian SC** — Senior Counsel. Joined Erin's appeal team in approximately October 2025.

OTHER WITNESSES

- **Atkinson, Sally Ann** — Senior official, Victorian Department of Health. Led the department's investigation into the source of the mushrooms.
- **Baldwyn** — Ben's friend. Went to the movies and McDonald's with the children on the day of the lunch. Recalled seeing plates in the sink afterwards. Name changed to protect privacy.
- **Canty, Darren** — Operations Manager, Koonwarra Transfer Station. Reviewed CCTV footage and directed an employee to retrieve the dehydrator from the e-waste skip bin at police request on 4 August 2023.
- **Cripps, Katrina** — Child Safety Officer, Victorian Child Protection Service. Visited Erin at Monash Hospital and at her home.
- **Hosking, Jennifer** — Corrections Victoria, Sentence Management Division. Gave evidence at the plea hearing about Erin's prison conditions in the Gordon Unit.
- **McKenzie, Christine** — Retired pharmacist and former Senior Poisons Information Specialist. Found and posted death cap sighting at Loch to iNaturalist in April 2023.
- **Schonknecht, Troy** — Environmental health officer, Monash City Council. Physically searched fourteen Asian grocery stores across

three suburbs. Found nothing matching Erin's description.

ONLINE FRIENDS

- **Ali** — The only person outside her legal team to attend court in support of Erin during the trial.
- **Christine** — Told the court Erin had described Simon as "controlling" and herself as an atheist.
- **Daniela** — Told the court Erin had complained Simon put the church before her and the family.
- **Jenny** — Semi-retired social worker. Gave key evidence about the dehydrator and Erin's chats about hiding mushrooms in food.

ABOUT THE AUTHOR

Cheryl Warren is an Australian writer and researcher based in regional Victoria, where she lives with her husband and their dogs.

An avid true crime reader for over forty years, Cheryl is fascinated by the ever-evolving science of criminal investigation — forensics, DNA analysis, digital evidence — and by the deeper psychological question that sits beneath every case: What is it that drives apparently ordinary people to commit devastating crimes? That intersection of science and human behaviour is at the heart of her work.

She is drawn to cases where the facts are complex, the people are real, and the truth matters — stories that unfolded slowly, that resisted easy explanation, and that left communities searching for clarity long after the verdict. Her research process is grounded in court documents, judgements, forensic records, interviews, and verified contemporaneous reporting. She does not speculate where the record is silent, and she does not sensationalise where the facts are already devastating enough.

Fatal Lunch: The Death Cap Mushroom Murders is her debut book. It tells the story of a woman who had everything — a family, a community, a life that by all appearances was unremarkable — and who committed a crime so calculated and so devastating that it destroyed all of it. Three people dead. A fourth left shattered. A motive never established. And a question that still lingers: for what?

Cheryl is currently working on her second book.

www.ingramcontent.com/pod-product-compliance
Lightning Source LLC
LaVergne TN
LVHW052034200926
848481LV00005B/1673